Grandma's
Back to Basics All Natural More Than Just a Cookbook

Teresa Thompson

Enjoy!
Teresa Thompson

DORRANCE PUBLISHING CO., INC.
PITTSBURGH, PENNSYLVANIA 15222

ISBN# 0-8059-6286-7
Printed in the United States of America

First Printing

For information or to order additional books, please write:
Dorrance Publishing Co., Inc.
701 Smithfield Street
Third Floor
Pittsburgh, Pennsylvania 15222
U.S.A.
1-800-788-7654
Or visit our web site and on-line catalog at www.dorrancepublishing.com

Contents

Contents

Introduction

Allergies

No amount of research can measure up to one's own experience with allergies. The reaction may be minor or so severe that it may cause death if not treated immediately.

As a young teen, I recall having hives on the palms of my hands and the bottom of my feet. I never knew what caused it. Over the years I have experienced other reactions such as rashes, lesions, hives, and itching around the joint area. I would scratch until I drew blood. However scratching did not produce relief. I learned to put ice or a cold wet cloth on the irritated spot. This seemed to help.

The doctors I consulted told me I would have to go through the process of elimination to find out what I am allergic to. I kept a daily log of everything I ate and drank. I had to figure out what each dish contained to help determine what was causing these reactions.

I suffered a severe skin rash, which caused me to lose a layer of skin on my arms. This was a result of consuming a diet supplement drink which contained an artificial sweetener. Since that time, I have decided not to use anything containing artificial sweeteners. I have occasionally found it necessary to drink a diet soda if there is nothing else to drink; however, I suffer the consequences.

Water, which is our most important nourishment for our bodies, is treated with chemicals. I discovered this when I was troubled with a rash that turned in to hives and lesions. It would get better only to get worse again. My doctor even treated me for poison ivy. I ate only at home or at the same restaurant. Each time I was careful to write down everything I ate. During this time I read in the local paper that the city water had several chemicals in it. I looked at my list which contained water, coffee, and soup. Since these are all made with the same water I stopped drinking water and coffee and stopped ordering the soup when I went out to eat.

My hives and lesions cleared up. Some allergic reactions will clear up as fast as they appear although other reactions can stay with you for weeks. This is when determining the allergy becomes confusing. In this case the best thing to do is to refrain from eating the food that you suspect is triggering your allergic reactions.

A person should drink eight glasses of filtered water per day. If you have trouble drinking water add a little lemon juice or apple cider vinegar. I suggest you begin your day with a glass of water in the morning. You will be surprised what a glass of water can do for you; this is especially important if you are having bowel problems.

I had a water filter installed on my water system. Then I asked the restaurant that I frequent to put a filter on their water system. I feel that all restaurants, work places and households should put a filter on their water supply because the water is treated with the chemicals. The filter should remove chemicals, bacteria, odor, chlorine, metals, and hard minerals.

Children should be encouraged to drink filtered water and 100% fruit juices like orange, grapefruit, cherry, papaya, pineapple, tomato, and V-eight. It is also important for children to drink milk, certified pure raw milk, buttermilk, and herb tea.

Check labels on bottled water to make sure it is filtered and does not contain chlorine. If you are drinking water from a faucet let it run awhile. By doing so, this will help to clear the pipes of residue. Always use water from the cold faucet and heat it as opposed to using water from the hot water faucet. This is important because the hot water comes from the water heater where it has been sitting for some time.

The best emotional security a newborn can have is to be breast fed. This helps to give them a better start. It frustrates me to see a parent give a young child soda. Besides the artificial flavors, artificial sweeteners, and white sugar, four sodas contain as much caffeine as two cups of regular coffee. Children who drink a lot of soda over a period of time can go through the same symptoms such as headaches and nervousness that anyone who switches from regular coffee to decaffeinated would experience. If the child is allergic to milk try acidophilus, soy, or goat milk. Natural juices are also recommended.

Just when I thought I had it all figured out, I learned about MSG (monosodium glutamate). I had noticed over the years, that within twenty minutes after I ate at certain restaurants I would get severe cramps and diarrhea. I also noticed a light headed feeling and buzzing in my ears. I went to the doctor on many occasions and after numerous tests and x-rays they could not find anything physically wrong with me. MSG has to be one of the worst things that can be added to our food unbeknown. To a person who may be terribly allergic to MSG he or she could die from the allergic reaction before getting help.

My problem did not stop there. After eating at a Chinese restaurant I woke up in the night with severe chest pains. My stomach felt like someone had kicked me. My lips and tongue were swollen and I was short of breath. I also experienced heart palpitations and a rapid heart beat. Even my lymph nodes were swollen. I had no idea what was happening to me. It seemed as if I was having a heart attack. I ended up in the emergency room. The doctor asked me where I had eaten. He explained to me if I eat at a Chinese restaurant I should ask them to leave out the MSG. However, I was unaware that American restaurants also use MSG. Since I had no idea what MSG was I ended up in the hospital and the doctor's office several times. I have learned that employees at many chain restaurants do not know if MSG is used. This is because the food is shipped in. It is best if you ask for the manager because all foods are supposed to contain a label with the ingredients. If the manager cannot tell you if the foods contain MSG and you suspect you are allergic to it, do not eat at that restaurant.

Because I was unable to drink coffee due to the chemicals in the water, I began drinking regular soda. I was eating pastas and bread because I felt safe knowing that some cooks were adding flavor enhancers and preservatives to the food. Once again I was wrong. I had new itches and I was more frustrated than ever. I went on a bus trip and visited an old working mill. They were grinding wheat and showing how they sifted the flour and added a bleaching agent. They let it set to whiten the wheat. It was as if someone turned a light bulb on in my head. I thought to myself *that's it*! I immediately stopped eating white bread and white sugar. I gave up the soda that contains sugar as well as anything that was made with white flour and white sugar. It was such a relief to stop itching. Occasionally I still eat something I should not. When I start itching, it reminds me that I should not have eaten that particular food.

There are all kinds of unbleached flours such as soy, durum, semolina, rice, wheat, rye, spelt, and others. Spelt has a slight tan color; unbleached white flour is fairly white without the bleaching. Also, you can find unbleached sweeteners such as sorbitol, lactose milk, soya, xylitol, sucanat, barley, malt, and turbinado (raw unbleached sugar) on the market. You may have to go to a health food store for some of these. If they do not have what you want they are usually able to order it for you. Other natural sweeteners are honey, 100% pure maple syrup, 100% pure corn syrup, and molasses. I have also found all natural flavored pancake syrup made with real fruit juices, corn syrup, and fructose in the grocery store. The best oils to use are sesame, safflower, peanut oil, soy oil, sunflower, cold pressed vegetable oil, corn oil, walnut oil, canola, virgin, and extra virgin olive oil. Most of these can be purchased at the supermarket or the health food store.

Use whole grain cereals, brown rice, whole wheat flour, beans, fresh fruits and vegetables. It would be nice if you are able to raise your own fruits and vegetables. If this is not possible there are organic farmers and stores that carry organically grown produce. Natural foods may not necessarily be organic but would be the least processed and contain only natural additives such as salt, pepper, and spices. Eat fresh eggs, cheese, raw certified goat or cows milk, and yogurt; be sure to read the label on the yogurt because some contain artificial sweeteners. In addition, when a recipe calls for baking powder make certain you use aluminum free.

Packaged foods entail new problems because of additives such as flavor enhancers, thickeners, mold inhibiters, filler, artificial flavors, colors, and preservatives. Although food additives have been approved, they continue to cause concern as to whether they cause illnesses and cancer. No matter how careful you are, you may still eat something that has chemicals in it and you may or may not have a reaction. It depends on how many allergens you have in your system at the time. When you eat something that is not natural the histamines in your body act like little soldiers protecting your body. This is what causes a reaction and from my own experience it is possible to take an antihistamine after eating something that you are allergic to, then even if you are careful not to eat any of the forbidden foods you may still have a reaction. The reason is the allergens stay in your body for an undetermined length of time. I have also discovered that after having an allergic reaction it is best to eat small portions of all natural foods. Also drink plenty of filtered water.

Chemicals in our food are probably one of the worst allergies to deal with because so many of the pre-packaged or processed foods on the market contain some form of additives. It is possible to be allergic to one or all of them. The reason a person can eat certain foods all their lives and suddenly have a reaction is because the allergens build up in your body.

If you are truly interested in becoming healthy and chemical free, the first step is to go through your cupboards and throw out anything that is not 100% natural. Read on.

My Reason for Writing this Book

I am writing this cookbook not only for myself, but also for others who may have the same problems I have had. This book is also for anyone who wishes to eat healthier.

I have had to change my eating habits back to the good old days when they did not have processed foods, additives, preservatives, and things I cannot pronounce. Knowing what they are and what they are doing to my system I would like to share my book with other people who are experiencing the same reactions as I have and who do not know what is wrong with them. It is not normal to get a headache, blurred vision, shortness of breath, or cramps and diarrhea after eating. What you are probably experiencing is an allergic reaction to food additives. Whether it is a preservative or a flavor enhancer it can be dangerous. Anytime you eat something you are allergic to, even a few bites, it can be a lethal dose. I strongly advise anyone having any of the previous mentioned symptoms to see a doctor.

I began reading all labels. There are words on the labels that I cannot pronounce. I made up my mind that if I cannot pronounce it, I do not want to eat it. Also, if there are so many preservatives in an item that it can sit on a grocery store shelf for a month and on my shelf for a month or more after I buy it it cannot be healthy for me. This makes one wonder if the experts have ever thought of doing a study on children's diets and their behavior problems. Artificial sweeteners have been known to cause buzzing in the ears and other problems. Combine those reactions with reactions that MSG and other additives can cause and I wonder what these chemicals can do to a child? I know it is awful for me when I have reactions such as rashes, hives, itching, and weird feelings in my head. A child does not know what is happening and reacts according to how he or she feels. Although I do have my allergies under control, when I travel it is difficult. I therefore take chances that the food I eat will be safe.

When you think about it, a person eats a lot of chemicals in one day. In a cup of coffee, if the water is not filtered, you are getting chemicals from the water. If it is not naturally decaffeinated coffee you may be getting chemicals as well. If you have sausage with your eggs, most of the seasoning used in making the sausage contains MSG. If you have bacon, smoked sausage, or ham these contain nitrites. Eat white bread and you are eating the bleaching agent used to whiten the flour. There is bleached sugar in the jelly you put on your bread. Pancakes, unless they are made with buckwheat or some other unbleached flour, will also contain the bleaching agent. It is best to have a drink of real orange juice, apple juice, grapefruit juice, or a glass of tomato juice without ice. Eat an omelet or eggs with whole wheat or a multi-grain bread, home fries, or hash browns. If you must eat meat have a pork chop or steak; be sure to ask if they use MSG to flavor the meat or if it is added to the fried potatoes. Use honey on your toast if the restaurant does not carry the jelly and jams that are made with honey and fructose. Use honey in your coffee instead of the packets of bleached sugar or the artificial sweeteners. Drink the coffee or tea only if the restaurant filters the water.

For lunch, if you have a sandwich, it would be best to eat where you can choose dark bread, whole wheat, or a multi-grain. Eat at places where salads have not been sprayed with preservatives. Ask for homemade dressings that do not contain a lot of additives. Do not order a low-fat hamburger as this may contain MSG. Check this out when purchasing low fat hamburger at the store. Lunchmeats contain nitrites and sodium phosphates. If you are considering having soup, ask if they put MSG in it, if they use a soup starter with MSG, or if they used any canned broth or soup.

Most canned soup or broth has MSG in it. Creamed or cheese soups (made fresh without MSG) would be best because these do not have as much water as would chicken soup or beef vegetable. There are some healthy soups that do not have preservatives. You should be able to find these at most grocery stores.

It is always safe to use apple cider vinegar and oil for your salad. Carry packets of unbleached sugar with you if you need to sweeten your salad or coffee. Also, health food stores carry packets of an herb sweetener extracted from the stevia plant. This sweetener does not have any calories and is all-natural. Health food stores carry regular and safely decaffeinated coffee, postum, cappuccino, and many flavors of teas.

Although I have been in eating places that used MSG in almost everything, most of them have something that I can eat. It is best to ask if an establishment uses MSG as soon as you get in the door. I am hoping that more people will do this and let restaurant owners know that we do not like preservatives and other chemicals used in our food. I have found that small hometown restaurants that cook from scratch are less likely to use preservatives and flavor enhancers. These restaurants use salt and pepper and natural flavorings. Many of the top restaurants also use these flavorings as well. They know what to use to make food taste good without adding chemicals and artificial flavorings. Some restaurants have prepackaged foods shipped in and a lot of the food has preservatives added for safety.

At dinner, you may choose salad or vegetables, as long as you have asked about MSG. Avoid breaded meats and gravies. If a restaurant uses MSG on their meats ask them if they can prepare yours without. Most of the time they can. Ask for real butter and sour cream for your potato. I also advise not eating the skin because potatoes are often sprayed with a chemical for storage so they do not sprout. If you wish to raise your own or know a neighbor that raises potatoes ask to purchase some before they are sprayed. Buy enough potatoes for the winter and store them in a cool place.

Desserts are made with bleached flour and bleached sugar so I usually avoid these dishes. Even a cheesecake, which is mostly cheese, will contain bleached sugar. If you read the label on ice cream, many contain carrageenan, ethyl acetate, and sugar which is bleached. Try making your own ice cream in your refrigerator freezer. It is rather easy. You just give it a stir now and then before it freezes.

I have noticed a few soup and bread eateries popping up where they filter their water, use unbleached sugar, honey, real half and half, unbleached coffee filters, and unbleached napkins. These establishments are great, but be careful because they serve lunchmeat. Lunchmeat contains additives. Ask for whole grain bread or bread that is made with unbleached flour. Order meat that is cooked on the premises like chicken or roast beef.

I am amazed at the reaction I get from waiters and waitresses when I ask if they use MSG. Some people have never heard of it.

I do not understand how a product label can claim to be "all natural" when it contains MSG or bleached sugar and flour. It seems as though some of our food is processed to the point of not containing any more nourishment than a piece of cardboard; then flavorings, monodiglicerides, pyrophosphates, sulfites, emulsifiers, preservatives, enhancers, stabilizers, ethyl acetate, carrageenan, and yellow dye #5 are added. Always read the label. It is amazing how many chemicals are put in our food.

I know it will not be easy to completely stay away from chemicals. However, I want to ensure that everyone is aware that the foods we eat every day contain numerous additives. If you are one of the people that may be having allergic reactions to food you may want to eliminate suspected foods from your diet.

In my recipe file you will find a fine assortment of foods that are tasty and healthy. I have included plenty of desserts, ice cream and candy recipes for the sweet tooth. Plenty of salads, vegetables, casseroles, breads, and dumplings are also included.

Some of you may gasp when you see a recipe that calls for lard. Lard is the only solid shortening that is all natural. You can buy it at a slaughterhouse or render it yourself saving the cracklings for biscuits, pie dough, soups and many other uses. Some stores still carry it. Look for pure lard with no additives. The recipes that call for lard are mostly cookies, cakes, and pie crust. Lard makes cakes moist, cookies softer. It is the best shortening for flaky pie crusts.

In my recipes that call for vinegar I use apple cider vinegar. It is fermented apple juice and you can make it yourself if you like. There are other gourmet vinegars on the market if you care to indulge. Because white vinegar is made from industrial alcohol, I save it for cleaning purposes. It is great for washing windows; I also use it in my laundry rinse water.

In place of bleached sugar I use unbleached sugar (turbinado) which is cane sugar that is processed to the point just before it gets the bleaching agent. I also like to use coarse raw sugar for sprinkling on top of cookies, cakes, and pie crusts. You can use it like any other sugar in most other recipes. I prefer using sorbitol or fructose to make lemonade, white frosting, or lemon meringue pie. The slight caramel flavor in the raw sugar gives lemon pie an orange flavor and a tan color. There are other natural sweeteners in the health food stores. You may substitute any of the dry sweeteners for one another or the same with the syrup type like molasses, honey, and corn syrup.

Remove outer leaves of lettuce and cabbage to get rid of chemicals. Make certain to wash thoroughly vegetables and fruits in filtered water that has a little apple cider vinegar added to it. Do not use precut, pre packaged lettuce or cabbage. It was probably sprayed to retard browning and to keep it fresh.

Although they do have pastas that are made with semolina flour, some pastas do contain mononitrates. It is best to make your own. If you care to purchase an electric pasta machine, simply put all the ingredients in the machine and turn it on. It makes all shapes of noodles and pastas. Some supermarkets also carry an all-natural pasta in a special section. You may have to ask for it. Some stores carry all-natural dry pastas made with semolina flour without the mononitrates.

When cooking at home you can enjoy breaded meats and gravies without the worry of MSG. You can also enjoy bread and desserts without the bleaching agents. You may not be able to buy fresh (seasoned) pork sausage in the store because they use a prepackaged seasoning that contains MSG. Therefore they are unable to leave it out. Buy pork roast and have the store butcher grind it for you. You can season it yourself. If the butcher cannot grind the pork for you consider finding a slaughterhouse or meat locker that will grind it for you. They may be able to season it for you without the MSG. With the smokers they have now you can smoke your own hams, turkeys, bacon, and fish.

Now for my recipes. Enjoy! Watch for my **Suggestions, Hints, Comments and Variations.**

Appetizers

(Snacks and Whatnot)

Cheese Ball

Crackers and Pecans

Crab Salad

Croutons

Mixed Nuts, Sugared Walnuts

Mixed up Snack, Pretzels with Hot Mustard

Onion Bloomer

Sourdough Appetizer

Tomato Bread, Garlic Bread

Wings (Honey Soy Style)

Cheese Ball

1 (8 ounces) package cream cheese, softened
4 cups shredded natural Cheddar cheese, softened
2 tablespoons half and half
2 tablespoons finely chopped sweet onion
2 tablespoons Worcestershire sauce
1/4 teaspoon Cajun seasoning
1/2 cup blue cheese, crumbled
1/4 teaspoon garlic powder
1/2 cup pecans, chopped

Mix all ingredients except pecans. Form a ball and roll in the pecans until coated. Serve with carrot sticks, bread strips or wheat crackers.

Crackers and Pecans

Wheat crackers (enough to cover a 10x15 inch pan)
1/2 cup butter
1/2 cup unbleached sugar
1 teaspoon pure vanilla extract
1/4 teaspoon ground ginger
1 cup chopped pecans

Place crackers on a foil lined 10x15 inch pan. Boil butter and sugar for 2 minutes. Add ginger and vanilla. Pour mixture over the crackers, sprinkle with pecans. Bake at 350° for 10 minutes.

Crab Salad

1 cup finely diced celery
2 cups flaked crabmeat, cooked and chilled
1/2 cup mayonnaise
1/4 cup sour cream
1/4 cup dill pickles, chopped
1 tablespoon minced onion

Combine all ingredients. Serve as an appetizer on wheat or rye crackers, all natural pig rinds or make miniature sandwiches. It can be served for lunch with potato salad and cole slaw with little toasted bread quarters. Note: Bread quarters are toasted bread slices and cut in quarters.

Croutons

3 cups cubed day old bread (homemade)
2 tablespoons butter, melted
1 tablespoons virgin olive oil
1/4 teaspoon garlic powder
1/4 teaspoon onion powder
1/4 teaspoon oregano
1/4 teaspoon basil
1/4 teaspoon sea salt

Mix all ingredients. Bake in a 300° oven for 15 minutes. Serve with appetizers, on salad, or in soups.

Mixed Nuts

1 to 2 tablespoons butter
1 cup fresh pecan halves
1 cup whole almonds
1 cup raw cashews
Sea salt

Melt the butter in a skillet over medium heat. Add the nuts and fry. Stir occasionally to coat the nuts. Continue frying until browned but do not burn. Remove from the heat and sprinkle with sea salt. Other combinations of nuts can be used.

Suggestion: Store nuts in refrigerator to keep them fresh.

Suggestion: Add a little sugar with the nuts when grinding them so they do not stick together.

Suggestion: To freshen nuts, fry in butter or heat in oven and add sea salt.

Sugared Walnuts

1/2 cup butter
1/2 cup unbleached sugar
1/2 cup brown sugar
1 teaspoon cinnamon
2 cups walnut halves

Melt butter. Add sugar and cinnamon. Cook until sugar is dissolved. Add nuts and stir until coated. Cool on cookie sheet.

Mixed Up Snack

3 quarts popped corn
2 cups small pretzels
2 cups mixed nuts
2 cups wheat Chex® (all natural or from health store)
1 teaspoon chili powder
3/4 teaspoon paprika
1/2 teaspoon garlic powder
1/4 teaspoon onion powder
1/4 teaspoon dry mustard
1/4 teaspoon cumin
3/4 teaspoon sea salt
6 tablespoons butter

Melt butter. Add seasonings. Pour over popcorn mixture.

Pretzels with Hot Mustard Sauce

1 egg
1/4 cup brown sugar
3 tablespoons unbleached sugar
1 teaspoon mustard
dash hot sauce (optional)

Mix all ingredients and cook until thick. Dip pretzels for a snack.

Onion Bloomer

1 large sweet onion
4 eggs
1/2 cup milk
1 cup unbleached flour
1 teaspoon sea salt
1/4 teaspoon red pepper

Trim top and outer skin of onion. Leaving the root end on to hold the onion together, slice it almost to the root. Put onion upside down in a large bowl of ice water. Let set for a few hours or overnight.

Mix flour, red pepper and salt together and set aside. Beat eggs and milk together. Dip onion into egg mixture getting as much as you can into crevasses. Remove excess. Dip onion into the flour mixture covering the onion as much as possible. Deep fry in hot grease at 350° until light brown. Tear petals from the onion and serve with dipping sauce.

Suggestion: Dip onion in scalding water for a few seconds before peeling. There will be fewer tears.

Dipping Sauce:
1/4 teaspoon cayenne pepper
1/2 cup mayonnaise
1/2 cup sour cream
seasoned Cajun salt

Mix mayonnaise, sour cream, cayenne pepper and seasoned Cajun salt.

Sourdough Appetizer

1 1/2 cups sour cream
1 (8 oz) package cream cheese
2 cups sharp Cheddar cheese, shredded
1/2 cup finely chopped sweet onion
1 teaspoon Worcestershire sauce
1 round loaf, sourdough rye, homemade bread
Fresh snipped parsley

Combine sour cream, cream cheese, Cheddar cheese, onion and Worcestershire sauce. Cook over low heat until cheese melts. Cut off top of loaf and hollow out bread leaving about an inch shell. Pour cheese mixture into the bread shell. Sprinkle with parsley. Cut bread (remove from inside of loaf) into cubes for dipping. Veggies and corn chips may also be used.

Tomato Bread

1 loaf homemade bread
1 (8 oz) package cream cheese
1/4 cup Parmesan cheese
2 tablespoons sweet basil
1/4 teaspoon sea salt
1 clove garlic
pepper
2 ripe tomatoes

Slice bread. Soften cream cheese to room temperature. Stir in the Parmesan cheese and the next four ingredients. Position the slices of bread onto a baking sheet that has a slight edge, slice tomatoes thin and place on the bread slices. Pour the cheese mixture over the slices. Broil for 5 minutes. Serve as an appetizer or with a pasta dish.

Garlic Bread

To make garlic bread, spread both sides of bread with garlic butter and fry in a skillet.

Garlic Butter: Place 4 cloves of garlic in an ovenproof dish. Drizzle with 1 teaspoon olive oil and sprinkle with sea salt and pepper. Cover with aluminum foil and bake at 400° for 20 minutes or until cloves are soft. Place 1 stick softened butter in a bowl with softened garlic cloves and beat until well blended. Store unused portion in a tightly closed jar in the refrigerator.

Garlic bread in the oven: Slice a loaf of French bread lengthwise and spread with garlic mixture. Bake at 375° for 15 minutes. May be wrapped in foil before baking.

Wings (Honey Soy Style)

1/2 cup apple cider vinegar
3 tablespoons honey
1 cup soy sauce
1 cup chopped sweet onion
2 tablespoons pressed garlic
2 pounds chicken wings

Heat vinegar. Add honey to dissolve. Add soy sauce, onion and garlic. Mix well. Stir in wings until well coated. Marinate for 2 hours, stirring occasionally.

Pre-heat oven to 400°. Arrange wings on two baking sheets. Reserve marinade for basting. Bake wings until tender and glazed, turning and basting occasionally.

Cook remaining marinade until slightly thickened and use as a dipping sauce. Use blue cheese dressing or hot sauce for dipping. Serve wings as an appetizer or a snack.

Blue Cheese Dressing:
1 wedge blue cheese, crumbled
small container sour cream
2 tablespoons cream or milk
Mix until smooth

Comment: Hot sauce for dipping can be made by adding a few drops of hot sauce to melted butter or to marinade.

Beverages

Cappuccino
Coffee
Iced Herb Tea
Hot Carob (Hot Chocolate)
Fresh Lemonade
Fresh Cider, Mulled Cider, Hot Spiced Cider
Health Drink
Nectar
Orange Whip
Punch
Banana Milk Shake
Strawberry Shake

Cappuccino

3 cups strong coffee
1/4 cup carob powder or cocoa
2 cups milk
1 cup half and half or cream
3/4 cup unbleached sugar
1 teaspoon pure vanilla

Combine and blend slightly in a blender. Serve.

Cappuccino (Espresso): 1 shot espresso and hot milk topped with whipped cream, cinnamon, or carob powder.

Iced Cappuccino:
1 cup unbleached sugar
1/2 cup carob or cocoa powder
1/2 cup instant coffee or postum
1 cup filtered hot water
6 cups cold milk
1 tablespoons pure vanilla
1/2 teaspoon almond extract
1 pint homemade vanilla ice cream

Mix first four ingredients. Stir in milk, vanilla, and almond extract. Cover and chill. Mixture can be kept in refrigerator for two days. Serve over ice or ice cream.

Suggestion: It may be better to buy all natural products like instant coffee, regular coffee, cocoa, carob, espresso, or postum from the health food store.

Coffee

Use 1 tablespoon coffee per cup plus 1 tablespoon for the pot. Perk, drip or automatic can be used. Serve with cream and unbleached sugar or honey.

Comment: If you are bothered with fibrocystic disease or pain in the breasts, you should eliminate caffeine from your diet. Use carob instead of cocoa or chocolate and drink naturally decaffeinated coffee.

Iced Herb Tea

Place 4 teaspoons of herb tea leaves in a tea ball. Place in a teapot with 4 cups boiling, filtered water. Let steep 3 minutes and pour over ice in a glass. Serve with lemon and unbleached sugar (optional).

Sugar Syrup: Dissolve 1 cup unbleached sugar or fructose in 1 cup hot filtered water. Store in refrigerator. Use to sweeten tea, juices and iced drinks.

Comment: Black or Green tea is very good for you.

Hot Carob (Hot Chocolate)

2 cups filtered, boiling water
2 cups scalded milk
pinch sea salt
3 tablespoons carob or chocolate
1/4 cup unbleached sugar
1 teaspoon pure vanilla
Whipping cream

Combine dry ingredients. Add hot water. Cook 3 minutes. Add milk. Pour in a mug and top with whipped cream.

Fresh Lemonade

1 cup fructose or sorbitol
1/2 cup filtered boiling water
1 tablespoon grated lemon rind
1 1/2 cups fresh lemon juice (8 lemons)
5 cups filtered water

In a large pitcher, dissolve fructose in hot water. Add lemon juice, rind, and cold water. Stir and serve over ice. Add a slice of lemon (optional).

Hint: Use fructose instead of unbleached sugar in lemonade. Unbleached sugar has a slight caramel color and flavor where fructose is more like white sugar but does not contain bleach.

Fresh Cider

Chilled fresh cider (unpasteurized) tastes the best. You can buy a juicer and make your own.

Mulled Cider
1 gallon apple cider
4 sticks cinnamon
1 teaspoon whole allspice
1 teaspoon cloves
1 naval orange, sliced
1 lemon, sliced

Add spices to cider. Cook for 45 minutes. Strain and serve hot.
Garnish with orange and lemon slices.

Hot Spiced Cider
2 quarts apple cider
1/4 cup unbleached sugar or molasses
1/2 teaspoon cinnamon
1/4 cup lemon juice

Heat and serve with lemon wedges and cinnamon stick.

Health Drink

1 quart natural apple juice
1 quart natural white grape juice
1/4 cup apple cider vinegar

Mix all ingredients together. Store in refrigerator. Drink one-half to one full cup per day. This is also a very good thirst quencher.

Nectar

1/4 cup orange juice
1/4 cup lemon juice
1/4 cup grapefruit juice
1/4 unbleached sugar or fructose
Pinch sea salt
1/4 cup filtered, hot water
Crushed ice

Combine juices. Dissolve sugar and salt in hot water. Add juices. Serve over crushed ice.

Orange Whip

1/3 cup fresh squeezed orange juice
1/2 cup milk
1/4 cup fructose or homemade powdered sugar
1/2 teaspoon pure vanilla
4 ice cubes
Combine and whip in blender.

Homemade Powdered Sugar: Use equal amounts of fructose or sorbitol and pure cornstarch.

Punch

2 quarts fresh orange juice
1 quart grapefruit juice
1 quart cranberry juice
2 cups mineral or sparkling water
1/4 cup fructose
Slices of orange and lemon

Dissolve fructose in juices, add water and fruit slices. Add ice cubes.

Suggestion: To prevent diluting the punch, place ice cubes in a tightly sealed bag before adding to the punch.

Banana Milk Shake

2 cups milk
2 ripe bananas
1/4 cup honey
1/4 teaspoon pure vanilla
2 drops banana extract (optional)

Place all ingredients in a blender. Blend well and serve.

Strawberry Shake

2 cups fresh strawberries
1 cup milk
1/2 cup half and half
2 tablespoons unbleached sugar or fructose

Put all ingredients into blender and blend at medium speed until smooth. Pour into glass and top with a sprinkle of cinnamon.

Variation: Replace milk with homemade ice cream.

Hint: Try an assortment of fruits or different fruits for a variety of flavors.

Breads

Yeast Breads

Bohemian Rye

Healthy Bread

Multi-Grain Bread

Oatmeal Bread

Potato Bread

Pumpernickel/Rye

Sourdough Starter with Yeast

Sourdough Pancakes

Sourdough Pizza Crust

Sourdough White Bread

Sourdough Cornmeal Bread

Yeast Breads

Before you start making your bread I have a few helpful hints to help you make the best bread.

First of all kneading the dough is hard to do but very important. It keeps you from adding too much flour. Add just enough flour to keep the dough from sticking to your hands. If you have a bread machine that is great. If your recipe is for two or more loaves then partially mix the dough, set the machine at the dough setting, cut the dough in half and let the machine do half of the dough at a time. Combine both halves once the machine is done. Continue to knead until dough does not stick to your hands. Form into two loaves and place in greased bread pans. Let the dough rise until it doubles in size and bake in oven.

Let the dough rise at least two to three times before baking, once or twice in a bowl or the machine and once in the bread pan. Three times doesn't hurt. It is best to follow the recipe.

Dissolve yeast in a little warm water with a little sugar to make sure it is good. It should bubble in 5 minutes. Never use hot water on yeast.

Gluten may be added to help bread rise. Use 1 teaspoon per cup of unbleached flour and 1 1/2 teaspoons per cup with whole-wheat flour or other whole grain flour. Be sure to sift gluten into the flour.

If you like a lighter bread add a teaspoon of baking powder to the dough.

Before baking bread, brush with egg whites or milk. This also helps seeds and salt stick to the bread.

If bread browns too fast, place it on the lower shelf and lay a strip of foil on the top shelf.

Lard is the best to use for bread when a recipe calls for lard or shortening.

Brush bread or rolls with butter after the bread has baked and is still hot.

Bohemian Rye

1 package yeast
1 tablespoon lard
2 cups scalded milk
5 cups rye flour (use 1 1/2 teaspoons gluten per cup of rye flour)
2 cups unbleached flour
2 teaspoons sea salt
1 tablespoon unbleached sugar
1 tablespoon apple cider vinegar
1 tablespoon caraway seeds

Dissolve yeast in a little lukewarm milk or water. Melt lard in the hot milk. Sift together flour, gluten, salt and sugar. Add half of the flour to the milk and lard mixture. Stir and mix well. Add the yeast mixture and stir in well. Add the vinegar and the remaining flour along with the caraway seeds. Knead until dough does not stick to your hands. Place in a large greased bowl and cover with a damp cloth. Let the dough rise until it doubles in size. Knead for a few minutes. Form into a round loaf. Let dough rise to double in size. Bake on a greased pizza pan. Bake at 450° for 15 minutes. Lower temperature to 375° for 45 minutes. Bread should sound hollow when you tap your fingers on it. Brush with melted butter.

Suggestion: Bread may be baked in a greased loaf pan.

Suggestion: Always add the last 2 cups of flour, a little at a time, in case you do not need all of it. Once the dough no longer sticks to your hands and you have kneaded it for several minutes, do not add any more flour. If you have added all the flour and the dough is still sticky, add a little flour to the board as you knead the dough.

Hint: To freshen bread, sprinkle it with a few drops of water, place in a paper bag and heat in the oven at 325° for 20 minutes.

Healthy Bread

4 cups unbleached flour
2 teaspoons sea salt
2 packages yeast
1 cup filtered warm water
1/2 cup honey
2 tablespoons canola oil
1 cup cottage cheese
4 egg whites
1 1/2 cups wheat flour (add approximately 2 1/2 teaspoons gluten)
1/2 cup wheat germ
1/2 cup old fashioned oats

Combine 2 cups flour, salt and yeast. Dissolve honey in warm water and add oil. Stir in cottage cheese and add to flour mixture. Add egg whites to the flour mixture and blend at low speed, beat for 3 minutes at medium speed. Add whole-wheat flour, gluten, wheat germ, oats and enough of the remaining unbleached flour to make soft dough. Knead until the dough does not stick to your hands. Place in a large greased bowl, cover with a damp cloth and let rise to double in bulk. Punch down. Let set for 30 minutes and form into two loaves. Place into two loaf pans, cover and let rise to double. Bake at 375° for 40 minutes or until done.

Suggestion: Use leftover bread for croutons, French toast, breadcrumbs, and stuffing.

Suggestion: Add leftover breadcrumbs to scrambled eggs.

Suggestion: Add lemon juice to recipes that call for whole-wheat flour or use gluten, to help it rise. It is not necessary to use gluten in unbleached flour.

Multi-Grain Bread

2 teaspoons plus 1/4 cup honey
1/2 cup warm filtered water
2 packages yeast
3/4 cup milk
1 egg
2 teaspoons sea salt
3 tablespoons butter
1 teaspoon apple cider vinegar
2 cups whole wheat flour (use 3 teaspoons gluten and sift together)
2 cups unbleached flour
1/3 cup natural wheat and barley cereal bits
1/2 cup rolled oats
1/2 cup sunflower seeds

Topping:
1 teaspoon sunflower seeds
1 teaspoon rolled oats
1 egg white

Stir 2 teaspoons honey, warm water and yeast in a bowl. Let stand for 5 minutes. Stir 1/4 cup honey, milk, egg and salt together. Add butter and heat on low. Cool. Add vinegar, 2 cups wheat flour and mix until smooth. Add wheat and barley cereal, oats, and sunflower seeds. Stir until well mixed. Add remaining flour. Knead 15 minutes. Place in a greased bowl. Cover and let rise to double. Punch down and let rise 20 minutes. Shape into a round loaf. Let rise to double. Brush bread with egg white and sprinkle with sunflower seeds and oats. Bake at 375° for 35 minutes or until done.

Oatmeal Bread

1 1/2 cups boiling filtered water
1 tablespoons lard
2 teaspoons sea salt
1 cup rolled oats
1 pkg yeast
3/4 cup warm filtered water
1/4 cup molasses
1/4 cup light brown sugar
5 cups unbleached flour

Combine hot water, lard and salt. Stir in rolled oats. Cool mixture until it is lukewarm. Soften yeast in warm water, set aside for 5 minutes. Add molasses, brown sugar, 1 cup flour and beat until smooth. Add rolled oats mixture and enough flour to make a stiff dough. Knead until smooth. Place in a greased bowl. Cover with a damp cloth. Let rise to double in size. Separate dough into two equal parts. Let rise for 30 minutes. Shape into two loaves and place into greased loaf pans. Brush top of loaves with melted lard. Let rise to double. Bake at 400° for 45 minutes.

Potato Bread

1 1/2 teaspoons yeast
1 1/4 tablespoons unbleached sugar
1/2 cup potato water
2 1/2 tablespoons lard
1/2 cup mashed potatoes
1 egg
2/3 teaspoon sea salt
1 teaspoon baking powder
2 1/2 cups unbleached flour

Dissolve yeast and sugar in 1/4 cup warm potato water. Melt lard in remaining 1/4 cup potato water. Add mashed potatoes, egg and salt. Stir in 1 cup flour. Mix well and gradually add remaining flour and baking powder. Knead for 15 minutes. Place in greased bowl. Cover and let rise to double in size. Punch down. Let stand for 20 minutes. Form into a loaf and place in a greased loaf pan. Let rise to double. Bake at 350° for 35 minutes or until done. Brush with butter.

Comment: This recipe is a good one for first time bread bakers.

Comment: This bread can also be made in bread machine. Dissolve yeast in a little warm (not hot) water first. This seems to work better.

Suggestion: Bread should always have a tan crust when done. If it seems to be browning too fast, bake on a lower rack and lay a sheet of foil on the top rack.

Suggestion: Place bread in a container while still slightly warm to keep a soft crust.

Suggestion: Place a pan of water in the oven while baking bread to keep crust soft.

Pumpernickel/Rye

Pumpernickel Dough: (First part)
2/3 cup warm filtered water
1/2 teaspoon unbleached sugar
1 package yeast
1 cup + 2 tablespoons unbleached flour
3/4 cup rye flour
1 1/2 teaspoon sea salt
2 teaspoons espresso coffee (health food store)
2 tablespoons carob powder or cocoa powder
1 tablespoon apple cider vinegar
2 tablespoon molasses

Dissolve yeast and sugar in 1/3 cup warm water. Combine salt, espresso and cocoa. Add vinegar and molasses to remaining 1/3 cup warm water. Stir in rye flour and yeast mixture. Mix well and add the remaining flour. Knead for 15 minutes. Cover and let rise to double in bulk. Now mix the rye portion of the loaf.

Rye dough: (Second part)
2/3 cup warm filtered water
1/2 teaspoon unbleached sugar
1 package yeast
1 cup + 2 tablespoons unbleached flour
3/4 cup rye flour
1 1/2 teaspoon sea salt
1 teaspoon caraway seeds
1 tablespoons apple cider vinegar
2 tablespoons molasses

Follow directions for pumpernickel eliminating the espresso and cocoa. Mix in caraway seeds before adding the remaining flour. Place in a greased bowl allow dough to rise double in size. Punch down both pumpernickel and the rye dough. Let them both sit for 30 minutes. Roll out both dough masses to an 11" x 8" rectangle. Place pumpernickel on top of rye. Roll dough together. Place in a large, greased bread pan. Let rise to double in size. Brush top with egg white and caraway seed mixture. Bake at 350° for 35 minutes or until done.

Caraway seed/egg white mixture: Beat 2 egg whites until frothy, add 1/2 teaspoon caraway seed, then brush on top of loaf.

Sourdough Starter with Yeast

1 package yeast
2 cups warm filtered water
2 cups unbleached flour

Mix well. Let stand uncovered in a glass container two days. Stir two or three times. Store covered in a refrigerator. Replenish with equal parts of water and flour. Yeast cells reproduce from old starter. Before using, let stand at room temperature until bubbly. Cover and return unused portion to the refrigerator.

Sourdough Pancakes

2 cups sourdough starter
1 teaspoon sea salt
1/3 cup unbleached sugar
2 cups unbleached flour
Filtered water
1 teaspoon baking soda
1 egg
1 tablespoon melted shortening

To make the batter combine sourdough starter, salt, sugar, flour and enough water to make a pancake batter. Let mixture sit out overnight. Reserve 2 cups batter in refrigerator for the next time. The next day add baking soda, egg and shortening. Fry on greased grill or in a frying pan.

Sourdough Pizza Crust

1 1/4 warm filtered water
3/4 cup sourdough starter
2 1/4 tablespoons olive oil
3/4 teaspoon salt
3 cups unbleached flour
1 1/2 teaspoons yeast

Dissolve yeast in warm water. Let sit 5 minutes. Add 1 cup flour, sour dough starter, olive oil, and salt. Mix well. Add remaining flour. Knead dough for 15 minutes. Let rise. Punch down. Allow dough to rest for 20 minutes. Roll out to fit pizza pan. Let rise for 10 minutes. Top with your favorite topping. Bake 350° for 20 minutes or until done.

Sourdough White Bread

1 cup sourdough starter
2/3 cup warm milk
2 tablespoons butter softened
2 tablespoons unbleached sugar
1 tablespoon sea salt
3 cups unbleached flour
1 1/2 teaspoons yeast

Dissolve yeast in warm milk. Add sourdough starter, butter, sugar, salt. Add flour 1 cup at a time. Knead 15 minutes. Let rise until double in bulk. Punch down. Let rest 20 minutes. Form into a loaf and place in greased bread pan. Let rise to double. Bake at 375° for 40 minutes. Brush with butter.

Wheat Bread: Replace 1 cup of the unbleached white with 1-cup whole wheat.

Hint: To speed up bread rising, place on top of hot oven or heat oven. You may also heat the oven slightly then shut if off and place dough in the warm oven to rise. This helps in the winter.

Hint: You may use bakers yeast. It will keep in the freezer making it easier to keep on hand.

Suggestion: Add lemon juice to recipes that call for whole-wheat flour. You may use gluten to help it rise.

Suggestion: When making cutouts for tiny sandwiches it is easier to freeze the slices of bread first.

Sourdough Cornmeal Bread

1 cup sourdough starter
1 cup milk
1 egg
1 1/2 tablespoons butter
1/4 teaspoon sea salt
1 cup cornmeal
2 cups unbleached flour
1 1/2 teaspoons yeast

Follow directions for white sourdough bread.

Breads

Biscuits/Dumplings

Baking Powder Biscuits

2 cups unbleached flour
4 teaspoons baking powder
2 teaspoons unbleached sugar
1/2 teaspoon sea salt
1/2 teaspoon cream of tartar
1/2 cup lard or butter
2/3 cup milk or sour cream

Combine flour, baking powder, sugar, salt and cream of tartar. Cut in lard until crumbly. Stir in milk until blended. Roll out dough until it is 1/2" thick. Cut out with top of glass or a small cookie cutter. Place on an ungreased cookie sheet. Bake at 450° for 10 minutes.

Hint: Lard makes flaky biscuits.

Suggestion: Add teaspoon cayenne pepper and 1/2 cup shredded Cheddar cheese to the dough.

Orange Biscuits

3 cups unbleached flour
4 teaspoons baking powder
1 teaspoon sea salt
3 tablespoons unbleached sugar, divided
1 tablespoon lard
1 cup milk or sour cream
2 tablespoons butter, melted
Rind (grated) and juice from 1 orange

Combine flour, baking powder, salt and 1 tablespoon sugar. Cut in lard. Add milk to form a soft dough. Knead on floured board. Press or roll out dough so it is 1/2" thick. Spread with melted butter. Dissolve 2 tablespoons sugar in orange juice. Spread on buttered dough. Sprinkle with grated orange rind. Roll up like a jellyroll and cut 1/2" thick slices. Place on greased cookie sheet. Let stand 10 minutes and bake in 450° oven for 15 minutes.

Biscuit Mix

8 cups unbleached flour
1 1/2 cups powdered buttermilk (from health food store)
4 tablespoons baking powder
3 tablespoons unbleached sugar
2 teaspoons sea salt
2 teaspoons cream of tartar
1 teaspoon baking soda
2 1/3 cups lard

Combine flour, buttermilk powder, baking powder, sugar, salt, cream of tartar, and baking soda. Cut in lard. Refrigerate until used. Mixture will keep up to three months. Do not add water until ready to use. Add 7 tablespoons filtered water to 2 cups mix. Mix well and turn onto a floured board. Roll out and cut. Bake at 375° for 25 minutes.

Suggestion: Add 1 teaspoon of unbleached sugar and a little yeast to the mixture. This will make the dough raise better.

Suggestion: Add 1 tablespoon celery seeds, poppy seeds, or sesame seeds to the dough.

Drop Dumplings

2 cups unbleached flour
3 teaspoons baking powder
1/2 teaspoon sea salt
1 tablespoons lard
3/4 cup milk

Combine flour, baking powder and salt. Cut in lard. Add enough milk for batter to stick together. Drop by spoonfuls into boiling liquid. Cover and cook for 10 minutes.

Never Fail Dumpling

1 cup unbleached flour
1 teaspoon baking powder
1 teaspoon sea salt
1 egg
1/4 cup milk
1 slice bread, cubed

Combine flour, baking powder and salt. Stir in egg, milk and bread cubes. Mix well. Let rise 2 hours. Knead down and let rise 10 minutes. Cook in boiling water for 10 minutes on one side, uncovered. Turn over and cook 10 minutes on other side with cover ajar. Cut with a string or pull apart with two forks.

** To cut a dumpling with a string, simply lay the dumpling on the string; wrap it as if you are tying a knot. This will cut the dumpling.

Breads

Cornbread/Muffins

Cornbread with Buttermilk

Corny Cornbread Sticks

Spicy Cheese Cornbread

Apple Bran Muffins

Blueberry Muffins

Nutty Onion Muffins

Upside Down Muffins

Cornbread with Buttermilk

2 tablespoons canola oil
1 cup corn meal
1 tablespoons unbleached flour
1/2 teaspoon sea salt
1 1/2 teaspoons baking powder
1/4 teaspoon baking soda
1 cup buttermilk
3 eggs

Heat oil in an 8" iron skillet or a muffin pan at 450° for 5 minutes. Combine cornmeal, flour, salt, baking powder and baking soda. Make a well in the center of the mixture. Blend buttermilk and eggs. Pour egg mixture into well of dry mixture. Stir. Pour into skillet. Bake at 450° for 20 minutes.

Variation: Add 1/2 cup cracklings to the batter. The cracklings should be ground first. Cracklings can be found at butcher shops, meat lockers, and some grocery stores in the meat department.

Corny Cornbread Sticks

1 cup unbleached flour
1 cup cornmeal
1 tablespoons baking powder
1 teaspoon sea salt
3/4 cup milk
2 egg yolks
1 tablespoon olive oil
2 tablespoons red bell pepper, finely chopped
2 tablespoons green pepper, finely chopped
1 1/2 cups corn kernels or an 11 ounce can, drained
2 egg whites
Jalapeno pepper (optional)

Combine flour, cornmeal, baking powder and salt. Stir in milk, yolks, and olive oil. Mix well. Stir in peppers and corn. Beat egg whites and fold into mixture. Spoon into a cast iron corn pan that has been oiled. Bake at 450° for 15 minutes.

Hint: To oil a cast iron skillet spread interior with oil and place in a hot oven for 5 minutes. A pan other than cast iron can be also used.

Spicy Cheese Cornbread

1 cup corn kernels
2 eggs
1 cup buttermilk
1/4 cup canola oil
1 cup cornmeal
2 teaspoon baking powder
3/4 teaspoon sea salt
1/2 cup shredded natural Cheddar cheese
1 1/2 tablespoons jalapeno peppers (optional)

Blend corn kernels in food processor. Add eggs, buttermilk and oil. Mix cornmeal, baking powder and salt in a bowl. Pour corn and egg mixture into dry ingredients. Fold in cheese and peppers. Spread into a greased baking dish. Bake at 375° for 30 minutes.

Apple Bran Muffins

3/4 cup unbleached flour
1/2 cup whole wheat flour
1 cup oat bran
1/3 cup brown sugar
2 1/2 teaspoons baking powder
1/4 teaspoon baking soda
1/4 teaspoon sea salt
1/4 teaspoon nutmeg
1/4 teaspoon cinnamon
1 cup sour milk
2 egg whites
2 tablespoons canola oil
1 cup peeled, shredded apple

Combine flours, bran, sugar, baking powder, baking soda, salt, nutmeg, and cinnamon. Blend milk, egg whites, and oil. Stir into the dry mixture just until moistened. Add shredded apples. Spoon 1/4 cup batter into greased muffin tins. Bake at 375° for 20 minutes.

Hint: May be stored in refrigerator, in an airtight container, for up to 5 days.

Hint: To easily remove muffins from tins, place muffin tin on a wet cloth after removing pan from the oven.

Blueberry Muffins

2 cups unbleached flour
2 tablespoons unbleached sugar
1/2 teaspoon sea salt
4 teaspoons baking powder
1 egg
2 tablespoons melted butter
1 cup milk
1 cup blueberries

Combine flour, sugar, salt and baking powder. Beat egg and stir in butter and milk. Add to the flour mixture. Fold in blueberries. Spoon into greased muffin cups and bake at 400° for 25 minutes.

Variation: Add 3/4 cup carob chips in place of blueberries.

Variation: Add 2 tablespoons canola oil and 1 cup shredded Cheddar cheese in place of blueberries.

Nutty Onion Muffins

1 1/2 cup unbleached flour
1/2 cup unbleached sugar
1 1/2 teaspoons baking powder
1/2 teaspoon sea salt
2 eggs
1/2 cup butter
1 1/2 cups chopped pecans
1 cup fine chopped sweet onion

Combine flour, sugar, baking powder and salt. Beat eggs. Melt butter. Add butter and eggs to flour mixture. Stir in nuts and onion. Fill greased muffin cups 3/4 full. Bake at 400° for 12 minutes.

Upside Down Muffins

Topping:
1/2 cup chopped pecans
1/3 cup brown sugar
2 tablespoons butter
2 tablespoons honey
1/4 teaspoon cinnamon

Combine all ingredients and divide in the bottom of 12 greased muffin cups. Set aside.

Muffin:
2 cups unbleached flour
3 teaspoons baking powder
1/2 teaspoon sea salt
1 egg
2/3 cup milk
1/4 cup honey
1/3 cup butter, softened
2 tablespoons grated orange rind.

Combine flour, baking powder and salt. Blend egg, milk, honey, butter and orange rind. Mix with dry ingredients. Spoon 1 tablespoon mixture into each muffin cup, containing the topping. Sprinkle raisin mixture over the batter. Add remaining batter and bake at 375° for 20 minutes. Cool 5 minutes and invert.

Raisin Mixture:
Mix 1/4 cup chopped raisins, 1 tablespoon unbleached sugar, and 1/2 teaspoon cinnamon.

Breakfast

Blintzes/Crepes/Pancakes/Waffles/Oatmeal Mixture

Blintz

Carob Crepes

Crepes with Sausage

Crepes Kids Love

Baking Powder Pancakes

Potato Pancakes

Sour Cream Pancakes

Buttermilk Waffles

Oatmeal Mixture

Blintz

1 1/2 cups milk
3 eggs
1 cup unbleached flour
1/2 teaspoon sea salt
1 tablespoons butter, melted
Olive oil for frying

Beat together milk, eggs, flour, salt and butter. Beat for 2 minutes. Heat a teaspoon of oil in a skillet. Pour 1/4 cup of the batter in the hot oil and immediately swirl the skillet to coat the bottom with the batter. Fry on one side then turn to fry the other side. Transfer to platter. Place 1 tablespoon blintz filling into the center. Fold in all four sides, turn over, and top with lemon honey sauce.

Blintz Filling:
Combine 1 pound small curd cottage cheese, 6 ounces cream cheese, 4 ounces goat cheese, 1/2 cup honey, 2 tablespoons cornstarch, 1 teaspoon grated lemon zest. Place in center of blintz and fold. Serve with lemon honey sauce.

Lemon Honey Sauce:
1 teaspoon grated rind from lemon, 1/2 cup filtered water, 1/3 cup honey, 1/3 cup lemon juice and 1 1/2 tablespoon pure cornstarch. Cook and spoon on top of blintz.

Carob Crepes

Mix 1 cup milk, 1/2 cup unbleached flour, 1/4 cup carob powder, 2 eggs, 1/4 cup unbleached sugar, 2 tablespoons melted butter and 1 teaspoon pure vanilla. Beat with mixer. Heat 1 teaspoon canola oil in a skillet and pour in 1/4 cup batter and swirl to spread out on bottom of skillet. Cook for 1 1/2 minutes and turn and cook. Place on a platter. Spread with cream cheese filling and roll up. Top with carob Frosting.

Cream Cheese Filling: Combine 3 ounces cream cheese, 1/4 cup sour cream, and 1 tablespoon unbleached sugar. Mix and spread on crepe and roll up. Serve with pure maple syrup.

Carob Frosting: Mix 24 ounces carob morsels and 4 cups heavy cream. Cook over low heat until thick. Remove from heat and stir in 1 teaspoon corn syrup. Chill for 2 hours and serve over pancakes.

Variation: Ricotta Cheese Filling: 1 lb ricotta cheese, 3 ounces cream cheese, 1/2 cup unbleached sugar, 1 teaspoon pure vanilla, 1/2 teaspoon sea salt and 1 teaspoon lemon juice. Mix and place in center of crepe. Fold over all four sides to make a square blintz or spread on crepe and roll up.

Variation: Heat 1cup pure maple syrup. Add 1 tablespoon butter and 1/2 cup chopped pecans or walnuts. Serve over crepes.

Crepes with Sausage

Crepe:
3 eggs
1 cup milk
1 tablespoon virgin olive oil
1 cup unbleached flour
1/2 teaspoon sea salt
Butter for frying

Beat eggs, milk and oil. Gradually add flour and salt, beat until smooth. Cover and chill for 1 hour. Coat bottom of skillet with melted butter. Pour 1/4 cup batter into the skillet and swirl around to coat the bottom of the skillet. Fry until lightly browned. Turn over and fry. Remove crepe and place on a platter. Fill with sausage mixture. Roll up and place in a baking dish. Bake at 350° for 15 minutes. Top with tomato topping.

Sausage Filling:
Blend 1 pound fresh ground pork, 1 teaspoon sage, 1/2 teaspoon marjoram, 1/2 teaspoon poultry seasoning, 1 teaspoon sea salt, and 1/2 cup minced sweet onion. Fry in skillet until brown. Drain. Add 1 cup shredded, natural Cheddar cheese and 3 ounces cream cheese. Stir until cheese melts. Place 3 tablespoons sausage mixture onto crepe and roll up. Place seam side down in a baking dish.

Tomato Topping:
Mix together 1/2 cup sour cream, 1/4 cup melted butter and 1/4 cup chopped tomatoes, place on top of meat filled crepe after it is baked. Sprinkle each crepe with 1 tablespoons shredded natural Cheddar cheese. Serve.

Crepes Kids Love

3 eggs
2 tablespoons olive oil
1 cup milk
2/3 cup unbleached flour
1 tablespoon unbleached sugar
1/4 teaspoon sea salt

Beat all ingredients together. Coat bottom of skillet with olive oil. Pour in 1/4 cup batter. Swirl to coat bottom of skillet with batter. Fry until lightly browned. Turn and fry. Place fried crepe on a platter and sprinkle with cinnamon and sugar mixture. Roll up and keep hot in oven until remaining crepes are cooked. Serve with whipped cream or pure maple syrup.

Suggestion: Crepes can also be filled with mixture of 3 ounces cream cheese, 3 ounces farmer's cheese and 1 tablespoons unbleached sugar. Blend well and spread on crepe. Roll up and top with a fruit topping.

Fruit Topping:
Combine 2 cups fresh fruit such as strawberries, blueberries or peaches. Cook with a little filtered water, add 1/2 cup unbleached sugar and 1 tablespoons pure cornstarch. Cook until slightly thickened.

Baking Powder Pancakes

1 cup unbleached flour
1 cup milk
1 egg
1 teaspoon baking powder

Mix and pour onto a hot greased griddle or skillet. Fry until brown on bottom and bubbly on top. Flip pancake over and fry until brown.

Suggestion: Stir remaining mixture periodically.

Suggestion: Add 1 tablespoons pure maple syrup to pancake batter.

Suggestion: Keep a shaker with cinnamon and sugar mixture in it.

Suggestion: To replace honey in a recipe, melt 1 cup unbleached sugar in 1/3 cup hot filtered water.

Suggestion: Try adding a 1/2 cup cornflakes, Wheaties, chopped nuts, or quick oatmeal to the batter.

Potato Pancakes

2 eggs
1/4 cup minced onion
2 potatoes, peeled and chunked
2 tablespoons unbleached flour
1/2 teaspoon sea salt
Dash pepper
1 tablespoons olive oil
Olive oil for cooking

Process eggs and onion in blender. Add potatoes and pulse until finely chopped. Stir in flour, salt, pepper and oil. Let stand for 15 minutes. Heat oil in skillet. Pour 1/4 cup batter into the skillet and fry on medium heat until brown. Turn over and fry until done (6 to 8 minutes). Keep warm in oven until ready to serve. Serve with applesauce or sour cream.

Sour Cream Pancakes

3 eggs
1/4 cup milk
3/4 cup buttermilk
3/4 cup sour cream
1 cup unbleached flour
1 1/2 teaspoons baking powder
1 1/2 tablespoons unbleached sugar
1/2 teaspoon sea salt
Olive oil for frying

Separate eggs. Blend egg yolks, milk, buttermilk and sour cream. Combine flour, baking powder, sugar and salt. Gradually add sour cream mixture. Beat egg whites into soft peaks and fold into batter. Heat oil in frying pan or griddle. Pour 1/4 cup batter onto hot oil and fry until pancake is full of bubbles turn and fry. Serve with maple butter syrup.

Maple Butter Syrup: Combine 1 cup pure maple syrup, 1/2 teaspoon cinnamon, 1/4 teaspoon ginger and 1 1/2 sticks butter in a saucepan. Cook on medium high heat to softball stage (236°) degree. Approximately 15 minutes. Pour into a bowl and mix until creamy.

Variation: Stir in carob chips. Heat oil in skillet. Pour in 1/4 cup batter. Fry until bubbly, turn and fry until done. Transfer to plate and top with raspberry sauce and whipped cream.

Raspberry Sauce:
1 1/2 cups fresh raspberries, 1/2 cup unbleached sugar, 3 tablespoons lemon juice, and 1/4 cup orange juice. Blend in food processor and sieve to remove seeds. Serve over pancakes and top with whipped cream.

Buttermilk Waffles

2 cups unbleached flour
1/4 cup light brown sugar
1 teaspoon baking soda
1 1/2 teaspoons baking powder
1/2 teaspoon cinnamon
1/2 teaspoon sea salt
3 eggs, separated
2 cups buttermilk
8 tablespoons melted butter
1 teaspoon pure vanilla

Combine flour, sugar, baking soda, baking powder, cinnamon and salt. Blend egg yolks, buttermilk, butter and vanilla. Stir into dry mixture. Beat egg whites stiff and fold into batter. Heat iron. Brush with oil. Pour 1/3 cup batter onto the iron and bake for 5 minutes. Serve with butter and maple syrup.

Variation: For cinnamon and sugar waffles, mix 1/4 cup unbleached sugar and 2 teaspoons cinnamon. Sprinkle on waffle batter before closing lid.

Variation: Butterscotch Sauce:
1 1/4 cups brown sugar
2/3 cup corn syrup
1/4 cup milk
1/4 cup butter

Mix all ingredients. Cook over medium heat for 20 minutes. Use on waffles or pancakes.

Oatmeal Mixture

6 cups quick oats
1/2 cup raisins
1/4 cup unbleached sugar
1/4 cup brown sugar
1 tablespoons cinnamon
1 teaspoon sea salt

Mix together all dry ingredients and store in airtight container.

To use:
Place 1/2 cup mixture into a microwave safe bowl with 3/4 cup filtered water. Microwave for 1 minute. Stir and microwave 1 more minute. Serve with cream and unbleached sugar or honey. If you prefer to use the stove, pour 3/4 cup filtered water into saucepan and heat. Add mixture cover and let set a few minutes. Add sugar and cream. Serve.

Breakfast

Egg Dishes/Omelets/Quiche

Coddled Eggs

Creamed Eggs

Hen-in-a-Basket

Scalloped Eggs

Asparagus Omelet

Broccoli and Egg Oven Omelet

Spanish Omelet

Scrambled Egg Casserole Quiche

Spinach Quiche

Zucchini Quiche

Coddled Eggs

6 eggs
1 1/2 cups milk
2 tablespoons melted butter
Sprinkle of sea salt
Dash pepper

Beat eggs until blended. Add milk. Pour into top of double boiler that contains melted butter. Cook over hot water, stir until thickened. Add salt and pepper. Serve at once on buttered toast.

Creamed Eggs

6 hard cooked eggs
4 slices toast (homemade bread)
2 cups cheese sauce
Sprinkle of sea salt
Dash pepper
Paprika

Slice eggs. Place on toast. Cover with hot cheese sauce. Sprinkle with salt, pepper and paprika.

Cheese Sauce:
Blend 2 tablespoons butter and 2 tablespoons unbleached flour. Stir in 1 egg, 3/4 teaspoon sea salt, 1/8 teaspoon pepper, and 1/4 teaspoon paprika. Add 1 cup hot milk with 2 tablespoons grated natural cheese. Cook until smooth and thick.

Hen-in-a-Basket

1 slice homemade bread
Butter, softened
1 egg
2 tablespoons hash browns
Dash sea salt

Butter both sides of a slice of bread. Cut a 2 inch hole in the center of the bread with a small glass. Brush oil on heated frying pan. Place bread in the pan on medium heat. Place hash browns in the center of the bread (hole) and break an egg and drop it in the hole. Fry until done on one side flip it over and fry the other side. When done place on serving plate and top with egg sauce. Fry the center to serve as a garnish with a sprig of parsley.

Egg Sauce:
1/2 cup butter
1 tablespoons filtered water
1 tablespoons lemon juice
Dash pepper
Sprinkle of sea salt
3 egg yolks

Melt butter. Add water, lemon juice, pepper and salt. Cook and mix a little of the hot mixture into the egg yolks. Blend and put egg mixture back into the hot mixture. Stir and simmer until thick. Pour over cooked Hen-in-a-Basket. Can also be served over cooked eggs.

Scalloped Eggs

6 hard cooked eggs
24 stalks of asparagus, cooked
1/2 teaspoon sea salt
1/8 teaspoons pepper
1 1/2 cups cheese sauce
3/4 cup buttered bread crumbs
2 tablespoons butter

Alternately arrange asparagus and egg slices. Season with salt and pepper. Add cheese sauce. Cover with breadcrumbs that have been fried in butter. Bake at 400° until sauce bubbles.

Cheese Sauce:
Blend 2 tablespoons butter with 2 tablespoons unbleached flour. Add 1 egg, 1/4 teaspoon paprika, 1/8 teaspoon pepper and 3/4 teaspoon sea salt. Stir and add to 1 cup hot milk and 2 tablespoons grated natural Cheddar cheese. Cook until smooth.

Asparagus Omelet

1/2 cup asparagus pieces
1 teaspoon butter
3 eggs
1 tablespoon half and half
Sprinkle of sea salt
Dash pepper
2 slices natural white cheese

Cook asparagus in a little filtered water. Melt butter in an omelet pan or skillet. Beat eggs and half and half, pour into the omelet pan and sprinkle with salt and pepper. When egg mixture is nearly firm add asparagus and cheese. Fold over and let set for 1 minute. Serve.

Broccoli and Egg Oven Omelet

10 eggs
1 1/2 cups broccoli, cut up
1 sweet onion, chopped
1/4 cup Parmesan cheese
2 tablespoons half and half
1/2 teaspoon sea salt
1 clove garlic, pressed
6 slices ripe tomato
1/4 cup Parmesan cheese

Beat eggs. Combine broccoli, onion, Parmesan cheese, half and half, salt and garlic. Stir in eggs. Pour into an 11x7x2 inch ungreased baking dish. Arrange tomatoes on top of mixture. Sprinkle with Parmesan cheese. Bake uncovered at 325° for 30 minutes.

Spanish Omelet

2 teaspoons butter
1 tablespoons chopped green pepper
1 tablespoons chopped onion
4 fresh mushrooms
sprinkle sea salt
dash pepper
1 or 2 drops hot pepper sauce (optional)
3 eggs
1 tablespoon milk
2 slices natural white or yellow cheese
3 slices ripe tomato
Salsa
Sour cream

Melt 1 teaspoon butter in a small frying pan. Add peppers, onions, mushrooms, salt, pepper and hot sauce. Fry slightly. Melt remaining butter in omelet pan or skillet. Remove vegetables with a slotted spoon. Beat eggs with milk and pour into the omelet pan or skillet. When eggs are nearly firm, add vegetables, cheese, and tomato slices. Fold over and let set for 1 minute. Serve with salsa and sour cream.

Scrambled Egg Casserole Quiche

1 pound ground pork, seasoned w/ sage
1 teaspoon sea salt
6 eggs, beaten
6 slices of bread (homemade), cubed
1 cup natural Cheddar cheese, grated
2 cups milk

Brown pork in frying pan. Add salt and seasoning. Stir in eggs, bread cubes, cheese, and milk. Mix well and refrigerate until morning. Bake at 350° for 40 minutes. Top with Hollandaise Sauce.

Hollandaise Sauce:
Put 1/2 cup butter in top of double boiler. Add 2 egg yolks and 1 tablespoon lemon juice. Cook over hot water, stirring constantly with a wire whisk until butter melts. Gradually add another 1/2 cup melted butter. Remove from heat. Stir in 1/4 teaspoon sea salt, a pinch of cayenne pepper, and 2 tablespoons cream. Serve over egg dishes.

Hint: If sauce curdles add 1 tablespoon cold filtered water and beat with mixer.

Hint: An easier method is to place egg yolks, lemon juice, salt, cayenne and cream in a blender and blend in hot butter. Make sure butter is very hot. Cook on medium until thick. Stir continuously.

Spanish Quiche

1 (10 ounce) package spinach, unsprayed
5 eggs
3/4 cup chopped green pepper
3/4 cup chopped onion
1 1/2 cups sliced mushrooms
2 cloves garlic, pressed
3 tablespoons canola oil
1 pound carton ricotta cheese
3/4 teaspoon sea salt
1/8 teaspoon pepper
1 tablespoon snipped parsley
1 (7 ounce) package Feta cheese

Wash and chop spinach. Beat eggs. Combine all ingredients and pour into a large baking dish. Bake at 350° for 1 hour or until firm.

Suggestion: It is best to wash vegetables with vinegar water in case they have been sprayed.

Zucchini Quiche

8 eggs
1/4 cup chopped sweet onion
1 1/2 cups shredded raw potatoes
1/4 cup Parmesan or natural white cheese, shredded
1 cup shredded raw zucchini
1/4 cup milk
1 teaspoon olive oil
Thin sliced zucchini
1/2 teaspoon sea salt
1/8 teaspoon pepper
1/2 teaspoon oregano
1 clove garlic, pressed
3 ounces Swiss cheese
1 cheese pastry shell

Beat eggs. Add onions, potatoes, Parmesan cheese, shredded zucchini, and milk. Pour into unbaked cheese pastry shell. Heat oil and fry sliced zucchini. Add salt, pepper, oregano and garlic. Place Swiss cheese on top of egg mixture in pastry shell. Add fried zucchini mixture. Baked uncovered at 400° for 20 minutes. Reduce to 350° until done. Total baking time is 1 hour.

Cheese Pastry Shell:
Cut 3 tablespoons butter into 3/4 cup unbleached flour. Add 1/2 teaspoon sea salt and 2 tablespoons cold, filtered water. Blend in 1 1/2 cups shredded, natural Cheddar cheese. Roll out and place in a large pie dish.

Desserts

Bars/Brownies

Lemon Bars

Energy Bars

Pumpkin Bars

Toffee Bars

Walnut Coconut Bars

Zucchini Bars

Banana Carob Walnut Brownies

Carob Turtle Brownies

Filled Peanut Butter Brownies

Fudge Brownies

Lemon Bars

1/3 cup butter
1 cup unbleached sugar
2 tablespoons unbleached flour
2 eggs
1/2 cup brown sugar
1/2 cup chopped nuts
3/4 cup shredded coconut
1/4 teaspoon sea salt
1/8 teaspoon baking powder
1/2 teaspoon pure vanilla

Cut butter into sugar and flour. Form crust by pressing into an 8x8x2 inch greased baking pan. Bake at 350° for 15 minutes.

Combine eggs, brown sugar, nuts, coconut, salt, baking powder, and vanilla. Mix well and spread over baked crust. Bake at 350° for 30 minutes. Frost immediately and cut into bars.

Frosting:
Mix until smooth 2 tablespoons lemon juice and 1 cup homemade powdered sugar. Spread on baked mixture and cut into bars.

Note: To make homemade powdered sugar mix equal parts fructose or sorbitol and pure cornstarch. Add more fructose if desired.

Energy Bars

1 cup quick oats
1/2 cup unbleached flour
1/2 cup grape nut cereal
1/2 teaspoon ginger
1 egg
1/3 cup applesauce
1/4 cup honey
1/4 cup brown sugar
2 tablespoons canola oil
1/2 cup golden raisins
1/2 cup dark raisins
1/4 cup shelled sunflower seeds
1/4 cup chopped pecans

Combine oats, flour, cereal and ginger. Stir in egg, applesauce, honey, brown sugar, and oil. Add raisins, sunflower seeds, and pecans. Mix well and spread into an oiled, foil lined 8x8x2-inch pan. Bake at 325° for 35 minutes. Cut into bars.

Pumpkin Bars

2 cups unbleached flour
2 cups unbleached sugar
2 teaspoons baking powder
1 teaspoon baking soda
1 teaspoon cinnamon
1 teaspoon nutmeg
½ teaspoon ground cloves
4 eggs
1 cup olive oil
2 cups prepared squash or pumpkin
½ cup chopped walnuts
½ cup raisins

Combine all ingredients, except the nuts and raisins, and beat for 2 minutes. Add nuts and raisins. Mix well. Spread into a greased 10x15x1-inch pan. Bake at 350° for 30 minutes. Cool and spread with frosting.

Frosting:
Combine ⅓ cup butter, 3 ounces cream cheese, 1 tablespoon milk, 1 teaspoon pure vanilla, and enough homemade powdered sugar to make a spreadable frosting.

Suggestion: If cooking your own pumpkin use squash instead of pumpkin. Pumpkin is quite watery and has to be cooked down for a long time.

Toffee Bars

1 1/4 cups unbleached flour
1 cup unbleached sugar
1 cup butter, softened
1 teaspoon pure vanilla
1 egg yolk
1 egg white
1/2 cups walnuts, chopped

Combine flour, sugar, butter, vanilla and egg yolk. Beat well. Spread batter into a greased jellyroll pan. Brush with egg white and sprinkle with nuts. Bake at 350° for 1 hour or until golden. Cut into bars and cool. When cool store in an airtight container.

Walnut Coconut Bars

1/2 cup butter, softened
1/2 cup brown sugar
1 cup unbleached flour
2 eggs
1 cup brown sugar
2 tablespoons unbleached flour
1/2 teaspoon baking powder
1/4 teaspoon sea salt
1 teaspoon pure vanilla
1/2 cup shredded coconut
1 cup walnuts, chopped

Mix butter, 1/2 cup sugar, and 1 cup flour until crumbly. Press into an 8x8x2-inch greased baking dish. Bake at 300° for 25 minutes. Mix together eggs, 1 cup brown sugar and 2 tablespoons flour. Add baking powder, salt, vanilla, coconut, and nuts. Mix well and spread over the baked dough. Bake at 350° for 30 minutes.

Zucchini Bars

3/4 cup butter, softened
1/2 cup brown sugar
2 eggs
1 teaspoon pure vanilla
2 cups shredded zucchini
1 cup shredded coconut
3/4 cup chopped nuts
1 3/4 cup unbleached flour
1 1/2 teaspoons baking powder
1/2 teaspoon sea salt

Cream butter and sugar. Add eggs, vanilla, zucchini, coconut, and nuts. Combine flour, baking powder, and salt. Incorporate into the batter and spread on a greased cookie sheet with sides. Bake at 350° for 40 minutes. Add topping.

Topping:
1 cup homemade powdered sugar (equal parts fructose and pure cornstarch)
2 1/2 tablespoons milk
1 teaspoon pure vanilla
1 1/2 tablespoons melted butter
1 teaspoon cinnamon

Mix well and pour over bars immediately after removing them from the oven.

Hint: More fructose can be added for a sweeter powdered sugar.

Banana Carob Walnut Brownies

1/4 cup butter
6 ounces carob chips
3/4 cup unbleached flour
1/2 cup unbleached sugar
1/3 cup chopped mashed bananas
1/2 teaspoon pure vanilla
1/4 teaspoon baking powder
1/4 teaspoon sea salt
1 egg
1/3 cup chopped walnuts

Melt butter and carob chips. Beat in flour, sugar, bananas, vanilla, baking powder, salt, and egg. Mix well and add nuts. Spread evenly in a greased pan. Bake in a 350° oven for 30 minutes. Cool and cut into squares.

Carob Turtle Brownies

2 cups carob chips
1 stick butter
3 eggs
1 1/4 cups unbleached flour
1 cup unbleached sugar
1 teaspoon pure vanilla
1/4 teaspoon baking soda
1/2 cup chopped pecans

Slowly melt 1 1/2 cups carob chips in butter. Remove from heat. Stir in eggs. Add flour, sugar, vanilla, and baking soda. Mix well and spread into a 9x13x2 inch greased pan. Sprinkle with remaining carob chips and pecans. Bake at 350° for 20 minutes. Drizzle caramel sauce over brownies.

Caramel Sauce:
2 cups unbleached sugar
1 cup filtered water
Caramelize sugar over medium heat until golden brown. Add water and cook for 3 minutes. Drizzle over brownies.

Note: To Caramelize means to fry in a skillet. Keep stirring mixture so it does not burn.

Filled Peanut Butter Brownies

3 eggs
1 cup butter
2 teaspoons pure vanilla
2 cups unbleached sugar
1 1/4 cups unbleached flour
3/4 cup carob powder
1/2 teaspoon baking powder
1/4 teaspoon sea salt
1 cup carob chips

Combine eggs, butter, and vanilla. Mix sugar, flour, baking powder, carob powder, and salt. Add to butter mixture. Stir in carob chips. Set aside 1 cup of the batter for the top of filling. Spread remaining batter in a 9x13-inch baking dish. Set aside.

Filling:
2 (8 ounce) packages cream cheese
1/2 cup peanut butter
1/4 cup unbleached sugar
1 egg
2 tablespoons milk

Beat cream cheese, peanut butter, and sugar. Add eggs and milk. Beat at low speed until combined. Carefully spread over batter in the baking pan. Drop the reserved batter by spoonfuls on top of the filling. Bake at 350° for 40 minutes. Sprinkle nuts on top if desired.

Fudge Brownies

1/2 cup butter
1 cup brown sugar
1/2 cup unbleached sugar
1/4 cup buttermilk
3/4 cub carob powder
2 eggs
2 teaspoons pure vanilla
1 cup unbleached flour
1/4 teaspoon baking soda
1 cup carob chips

Combine butter, sugars, and buttermilk. Cook and stir over medium heat, just to boiling point. Remove from heat and allow mixture to cool slightly. Stir in carob powder, eggs, and vanilla. Mix flour and baking soda together. Incorporate into cooked mixture. Beat mixture at least 25 strokes. Fold in carob chips. Spread evenly into a lightly greased pan (9x13-inch). Bake at 350° for 20 minutes. Do not over bake. Cool before cutting.

Desserts

Cakes

Angel Cake

1 1/4 cups fructose (sifted and measured)
1 cup unbleached flour (sifted and measured)
1 cup egg whites (8 to 10)
1 teaspoon cream of tartar
1/2 teaspoon sea salt
1 tablespoon filtered water
1 teaspoon pure vanilla

Sift flour and fructose separately. Measure after sifting. Whip egg whites until nearly stiff. Add salt, water, vanilla. Add cream of tartar. Continue to beat egg whites until they hold a stiff peak. Divide fructose into 4 parts. Add 1 part at a time to egg whites. Beat 10 strokes with a spatula after each addition. Divide flour into 4 parts. Fold in 1 part at a time. Folding 10 strokes after each addition of flour. Pour into a tube pan. DO NOT GREASE. Bake at 325° until light tan, about 50 minutes. Serve plain or with whipped cream or a boiled icing.

Boiled Icing:
1 cup fructose
1/3 cup filtered water
2 egg whites
1/2 teaspoon cream of tartar
1 teaspoon pure vanilla

Cook fructose and water until thread spins when spilled from a spoon. Beat egg whites and cream of tartar until stiff peaks form. Continue beating as you slowly add cooked water/fructose mixture making sure mixture hits the edge of the bowl and runs into the egg whites. Blend in vanilla.

Variation: Use cherry juice in place of water.

Variation: Use lemon extract in place of vanilla.

Carob Cake

2 cups unbleached flour
1 teaspoon sea salt
1 teaspoon baking powder
2 teaspoons baking soda
3/4 cup carob powder
2 cups unbleached sugar
1 cup canola oil
2 eggs
2 teaspoons pure vanilla
1 cup hot coffee or hot water
1 cup milk

Combine first five ingredients. Beat sugar, oil, eggs, and vanilla. Add to flour mixture along with coffee and milk. Mix until well blended. Pour into a greased and floured 9x13x2-inch pan. Sprinkle with coarse raw sugar. Bake at 350° for 35 minutes. Serve with ice cream.

Comment: All ovens vary so always check cake a little earlier.

Glazed Carrot Cake

1 cup fresh pineapple, crushed
1/4 cup unbleached sugar
2 cups unbleached flour
2 teaspoons baking soda
1/2 teaspoon sea salt
2 teaspoons cinnamon
2 cups unbleached sugar
3 eggs
3/4 cup canola oil
3/4 cup sour milk
2 teaspoons pure vanilla
2 cups grated carrots
1/2 cup fresh coconut, shredded
1 cup chopped pecans

Cook pineapple and 1/4 cup sugar for 2 minutes, over low heat. Drain and save syrup. Combine dry ingredients. Beat eggs, oil, and milk. Add drained pineapple, vanilla, carrots, coconut and pecans to the egg mixture. Stir until blended. Add dry ingredients. Mix well. Pour batter into 3 greased and wax paper lined, 9 inch round cake pans. Bake at 350° for 30 minutes. Drizzle sour cream glaze over layers. Cool for 25 minutes. Remove from pans.

Sour Cream Glaze:
Bring to a boil 1 cup unbleached sugar, 1 1/2 teaspoons baking soda, 1/2 cup sour cream, 1/2 cup butter, and 1 tablespoon reserved pineapple syrup. Stir and boil for 4 minutes. Add 1 teaspoon pure vanilla. Place 1 layer on cake plate and frost. Add second layer and frost. Add third layer and frost with remaining cream cheese frosting.

Cream Cheese Frosting:
Beat 3/4 cup butter, 2 (8 ounce) packages cream cheese, 2 cups homemade powdered sugar (equal parts fructose and cornstarch) and 2 teaspoons pure vanilla. Use enough milk to make a soft frosting. Beat until smooth.

Hint: Adjust sweetness of powdered sugar by adding more fructose.

Lemon Cream Cakes

1 cup butter, softened
2 cups unbleached sugar
3 eggs
1 teaspoon pure lemon extract
2 teaspoons grated lemon peel
3 1/2 cups unbleached flour
2 teaspoons baking powder
1 teaspoon baking soda
1/2 teaspoon sea salt
2 cups sour cream

Cream butter and sugar. Add eggs, lemon extract, and grated lemon rind. Combine flour, baking powder, baking soda, and salt. Add to egg mixture alternately with sour cream. Fill greased muffin tins or paper cupcake holders 1/2 full. Bake at 350° for 25 minutes. Cool and frost with lemon frosting.

Lemon Frosting:
4 tablespoons butter
2 cups homemade powdered sugar (equal parts fructose and pure cornstarch)
3 tablespoons lemon juice
1 teaspoon lemon extract
1/4 teaspoon grated lemon rind
2 tablespoons milk

Beat softened butter, powdered sugar, lemon juice, lemon extract, grated lemon rind, and milk. Use more powdered sugar or milk if needed.

Maple Nut Cake

2 cups unbleached flour
1 tablespoon baking powder
1 teaspoon baking soda
1 teaspoon cinnamon
1 cup softened butter
3/4 cup unbleached sugar
1/2 cup pure maple syrup
2 eggs
2 cups sweet potatoes, cooked and mashed
1 teaspoon pure maple extract
1/4 cup brown sugar
3/4 cup chopped nuts

Combine flour, baking powder, baking soda, and cinnamon. Cream together butter and sugar. Add maple syrup and eggs. Beat well. Stir in cooled sweet potatoes and extract. Beat until smooth. Blend in flour mixture and fold in brown sugar and nuts. Pour into 3 greased and floured layer pans. Bake at 350° for 25 minutes. Cool and frost with maple frosting.

Maple Frosting:
1/4 cup heavy cream
12 ounce package cream cheese
1/4 teaspoon pure maple extract
6 tablespoons butter
2 cups homemade powdered sugar

Beat heavy cream and softened cream cheese. Add maple extract and softened butter. Blend in 2 cups homemade powdered sugar. (equal parts sorbitol or fructose and pure cornstarch) or enough to make a spreadable frosting. More milk can be used if needed.

Oatmeal Cake

1 stick butter
1 1/4 cups boiling filtered water
1 cup oatmeal
1 cup brown sugar
1 cup unbleached sugar
2 eggs
1 1/3 cups unbleached flour
1 teaspoon baking soda
1 teaspoon cinnamon
1 teaspoon sea salt

Melt butter in hot water. Add oatmeal. Stir in sugars and eggs. Add flour, baking soda, cinnamon, and salt. Pour into a greased and floured 9x13x2 inch pan. Bake at 350° for 35 minutes. Frost with coconut butter frosting.

Coconut Butter Frosting:
1 cup brown sugar
1/2 cup condensed milk
4 teaspoons butter
1 cup shredded coconut
1/2 cup chopped nuts

Cook brown sugar, milk, and butter for 2 minutes. Add coconut and chopped nuts. Mix well and spread on top of warm cake.

Orange Cake

½ cup softened butter
2 cups unbleached sugar
4 egg yolks
⅓ cup orange juice
3 teaspoons grated orange rind
1 cup filtered water
3 cups unbleached flour
Pinch sea salt
3 teaspoons baking powder
2 egg whites

Cream butter and sugar. Add egg yolks. Beat. Add juice, rind, and water. Beat 1 minute. Combine flour, salt, and baking powder. Add to egg and sugar batter. Beat eggs whites until frothy and fold into the batter. Pour into a 9x13x2 inch baking dish. Bake at 350° for 30 minutes. Frost with boiled orange frosting.

Boiled Orange Frosting:
1 cup fructose
⅓ cup orange juice
2 egg whites
½ teaspoon cream of tartar
1 teaspoon pure vanilla

Cook fructose and orange juice until it spins a thread when spilled from a spoon. Beat egg whites and cream of tartar until stiff peaks form. Continue beating while adding the fructose/orange syrup. Add vanilla and blend. Spread on cooled cake.

Pineapple Cake

2 cups chopped pineapple
1/2 cup fructose
1 cup filtered water
2 cups unbleached flour
2 cups fructose
2 teaspoons baking soda
Pinch sea salt
2 eggs
1 cup chopped nuts

Cook pineapple, 1/2 cup fructose, and water. Drain. Save syrup for butter cream cheese frosting. Combine flour, fructose, salt, and baking soda. Add drained pineapple and eggs. Beat well and add chopped nuts. Pour into a 9x13x2-inch glass baking dish. Bake at 350° for 45 minutes. Spread with Butter Cream Cheese Frosting.

Butter cream cheese frosting:
1 stick butter
1 (8ounce) package cream cheese
1 tablespoon syrup from cooked pineapple
2 cups homemade powdered sugar

Cream softened butter and softened cream cheese. Add 1 tablespoon syrup from cooked pineapple. Add homemade powdered sugar (equal parts fructose or sorbitol and pure cornstarch) a little at a time to make a spreadable frosting. Use more of the syrup from the cooked pineapple if needed.

Poppy Seed Cake

2 3/4 cups unbleached sugar
1 cup olive oil
3 eggs
1 1/2 teaspoons pure vanilla
1 teaspoon apple cider vinegar
3 cups unbleached flour
2 tablespoons poppy seeds
1 1/2 teaspoons baking powder
1/2 teaspoon sea salt
1 1/2 cups milk

Beat sugar, oil, eggs, vanilla, and vinegar. Combine flour, poppy seeds, baking powder, and sea salt. Add to egg mixture alternately with milk. Beat until well blended. Pour into greased and floured bundt pan. Bake at 350° for 50 minutes. Top with orange glaze.

Orange Glaze:
Blend 1 cup fructose, 1/4 cup orange juice, and 1 teaspoon pure vanilla. Beat well and spoon over warm cake.

Suggestion: Do not eat food with poppy seeds if you are going to have a drug test. The test may show up with a positive reading.

Hint: Do not overbeat when using an electric mixer or your cake will be dry.

Raisin Cream Cake

1 cup unbleached sugar
1 cup sour cream
2 egg yolks
2 cups unbleached flour
1/2 teaspoon baking soda
1 teaspoon baking powder
1/2 teaspoon sea salt
1 teaspoon cinnamon
1 teaspoon nutmeg
1/2 teaspoon cloves
2 egg whites
1 teaspoon pure vanilla
1 cup chopped raisins

Beat sugar, sour cream, and egg yolks. Combine flour, baking soda, baking powder, salt, cinnamon, nutmeg, and cloves. Add to egg mixture. Blend well. Fold in stiffly beaten egg whites, vanilla, and raisins. Pour into greased layer cake pans. Bake at 375° for 30 minutes. Frost with almond butter icing.

Almond Butter Icing:
1 cup butter, softened
1 cup unbleached sugar
1 cup milk
4 teaspoons unbleached flour
2 teaspoons pure almond extract

Cream 1 cup butter and 1 cup sugar. Beat for 4 minutes. Cook milk and flour to boiling point. Cool and add butter mixture. Beat for 4 minutes and stir in almond extract.

Sour Cream Devil's Food Cake

2 cups brown sugar
1/2 cup lard
2 eggs
1 teaspoon pure vanilla
2 1/2 cups unbleached flour
1 tablespoon instant coffee (from health food store)
1/3 cup carob powder
1 teaspoon baking soda
1 teaspoon baking powder
1/4 teaspoon sea salt
1 cup sour cream

Cream sugar and lard. Add eggs and vanilla. Beat well. Combine flour, instant coffee, carob powder, baking soda, baking powder, and salt. Add egg mixture and sour cream. Beat for 2 minutes. Pour into greased layer cake pans. Bake at 375° for 25 minutes. Cool and frost with sour cream frosting:

Sour Cream Frosting:
1/2 cup carob powder
1/4 cup hot milk
1/2 cup butter
1/2 cup light corn syrup
1 cup whipping cream
1/2 cup unbleached sugar
4 egg yolks
Pinch sea salt
1/4 cup sour cream

Dissolve carob powder in hot milk. Add butter and corn syrup. Blend and set aside. Combine cream, sugar, egg yolks, and salt. Blend well. Cook and stir over medium low heat. Do not boil. Cook about 8 minutes until thickened. Add carob mixture and remove from heat. Stir until smooth. Mix in sour cream. Refrigerate until spreadable. If necessary, add homemade powdered sugar (equal parts fructose or sorbitol and pure cornstarch).

Sour Cream Rubarb Cake

1 1/2 cups brown sugar
1/2 cup butter
2 cups unbleached flour
1 teaspoon baking soda
Pinch sea salt
1 cup sour milk
2 cups rhubarb, diced fine
1/3 cup unbleached sugar (for topping)
1/2 cup coconut
1/2 teaspoon cinnamon

Cream brown sugar and butter. Combine flour, soda, and salt. Add to sugar and butter mixture alternately with milk. Stir in rhubarb. Pour into a greased and floured 9x13x2-inch baking dish. Mix together sugar, coconut, and cinnamon. Sprinkle on top of batter and bake at 350° for 45 minutes. Serve with whipped cream.

Hint: To remove air bubbles from cake batter before baking, hold pan with cake batter in it, a few inches above the counter and let it drop.

Hint: To make a heart shaped cake use your favorite cake batter and bake (1) 9-inch round cake and (1) 9-inch square cake. Cut the round one in half. Turn the square cake so it resembles a diamond shape. Place 1/2 of the round cake against each top edge of the square cake. Trim edges and frost.

Desserts

Coffee Cakes

Crunchy Blueberry Coffee Cake

Fresh Pineapple Upside Down Coffee Cake

Strawberry Rhubarb Coffee Cake

Squash Coffee Cake

Apple Crisp

Cream Puffs

Gingerbread with Cream Cheese

Gingerbread with Orange Sauce

Crunchy Blueberry Coffee Cake

1/2 cup butter, softened
3/4 cup unbleached sugar
2 eggs
2 teaspoons pure vanilla
2 cups unbleached flour
2 teaspoons baking powder
1/2 teaspoon sea salt
3/4 cup milk
1 1/2 cups blueberries

Cream butter and sugar together. Add eggs and vanilla. Combine flour, baking powder, and salt. Stir into egg mixture alternately with milk. Mix well. Pour 2/3 of the batter into a spring form pan. Sprinkle with 2/3 of the crunchy streusel topping mixture. Top with blueberries and remaining batter. Bake at 350° for 65 minutes. Cool 10 minutes before removing sides.

Crunchy Streusel Topping:
Combine 1/2 cup brown sugar, 1/3 cup unbleached flour, 1/2 teaspoon cinnamon, and 1/3 cup chopped pecans. Cut in 1/3 cup butter.

Fresh Pineapple Upside Down Coffee Cake

1/4 cup butter
1 cup brown sugar
Slices of pineapple (enough to cover skillet)
1/2 cup dried cherries
3 eggs, separated
1 cup unbleached sugar
1 cup unbleached flour
1 teaspoon baking soda
1 teaspoon sea salt
1/2 teaspoon cinnamon
1/3 cup buttermilk

Melt butter in a 10 inch iron skillet or other pan that can be put in oven. Sprinkle brown sugar in the melted butter. Arrange whole slices of pineapple in the skillet, placing cherries in between slices of pineapple. Cook until bubbly and pineapple is browned. Remove from heat. In a separate bowl beat egg yolks and sugar. Combine flour, soda, salt, and cinnamon. Add to yolk mixture. Beat until blended. Add buttermilk and stir. Beat egg whites until they are stiff but not dry. Fold into batter and spoon over fruit. Bake at 375° for 35 minutes. Loosen edges with a knife.

Strawberry Rubarb Coffee Cake

1 cup unbleached sugar
4 teaspoons pure cornstarch
2 tablespoons orange juice
4 cups fresh rhubarb
1 cup unbleached flour
2 tablespoons unbleached sugar
1 1/2 teaspoons baking powder
1/4 cup butter
1 egg
2 tablespoons milk
1 pint fresh strawberries (halved)
Cream

Combine 1 cup sugar and cornstarch in a saucepan. Stir in orange juice and rhubarb. Cook and stir until thick and bubbly. Remove from heat. Combine flour, 2 tablespoons sugar, and baking powder. Cut in butter. Stir together egg and milk. Add to flour mixture. Stir just until moist. Turn onto a floured board and knead for 1 minute.

Roll out to 11x4-inch rectangle. Cut lengthwise in 1/2 inch strips. Stir strawberries into rhubarb mixture. Pour hot fruit mixture into a rectangle baking dish. Weave strips of dough over the fruit mixture forming a lattice top. Trim edges. Place in oven on a foil lined cookie sheet. Bake at 400° for 25 minutes. Serve with cream or ice cream.

Squash Coffee Cake

½ cup butter
½ cup lard
1 cup unbleached sugar
2 eggs
1 cup butter cup squash (cooked)
1 teaspoon pure vanilla
2 cups unbleached flour
2 teaspoons baking powder
1½ teaspoons cinnamon
½ teaspoon baking soda
½ teaspoon sea salt
¼ teaspoon ginger
¼ teaspoon nutmeg
Pinch of cloves
½ cup unsweetened applesauce

Cream butter, lard, sugar, and eggs. Add remaining ingredients (except applesauce) and mix well. Spoon half of the batter into a 9-inch spring form pan. Spread with applesauce and half of the streusel topping. Add remaining batter and the remaining streusel topping. Bake at 350° for 1 hour. Let stand 10 minutes. Remove from pan and drizzle with glaze.

Streusel Topping:
Combine ¼ cup brown sugar, ¼ cup unbleached sugar, ¼ cup unbleached flour, ¼ cup rolled oats, ¼ cup chopped nuts, 1½ teaspoons cinnamon and 3 tablespoons softened butter.

Glaze:
Combine ½ cup homemade powdered sugar (equal parts fructose and pure cornstarch), ¼ teaspoon pure vanilla, 1 to 2 teaspoons filtered hot water or enough to make a drizzle frost.

Apple Crisp

4 apples, peeled and sliced
1 tablespoon lemon juice
1/3 cup unbleached flour
1 cup rolled oats
1/2 cup brown sugar
1/2 teaspoon sea salt
1 teaspoon cinnamon
1/3 cup melted butter

Place apple slices into an 8x8x2-inch greased baking dish. Sprinkle with lemon juice. Combine flour, oats, sugar, salt, and cinnamon. Add melted butter and mix until crumbly. Spread mixture over apples. Bake at 375° for 30 minutes. Serve with ice cream or caramel sauce.

Suggestion: Use other fruits as blueberries, pears, or peaches.

Cream Puffs

1 cup hot filtered water
1/2 butter
1/2 teaspoon sea salt
1 cup unbleached flour
4 eggs

Boil water, butter, and salt together. Add flour all at once. Stir in eggs one at a time. Drop by spoonfuls onto a greased baking sheet. Bake at 400° for 15 minutes. Continue baking for another 30 minutes at 350°. Cool and fill with whipped cream or custard. Serve immediately.

Éclairs:
Use pastry tube to make 4 inch strips. Bake. Fill with custard and drizzle with chocolate frosting on top.

Custard Filling:
Combine 1/3 cup unbleached flour, 1/2 cup unbleached sugar, and 1/2 teaspoon sea salt. Stir in 2 cups milk. Cook over medium heat. Stir constantly. Beat 2 eggs and stir half of the hot mixture into the eggs. Mix thoroughly. Pour mixture back into the pan and cook until thick. Cool slightly and add 2 teaspoons vanilla. Use in pies, cream puffs, and éclairs.

Chocolate Frost:
Melt together 1/2 cup butter, 2/3 cup carob powder, 1/4 cup cream, 1 teaspoon pure vanilla, and enough homemade powdered sugar to make it spreadable. If you prefer to drizzle, add more cream.

Gingerbread with Cream Cheese

1 1/2 cups unbleached flour
1 teaspoon cinnamon
1 teaspoon grated ginger root or 1/2 teaspoon ginger
3/4 teaspoon baking soda
1/2 teaspoon baking powder
1/2 cup butter
1/4 cup brown sugar
1/2 cup molasses
1 egg
1/2 cup buttermilk or sour milk
Raw sugar for sprinkle

Batter:
Combine flour, cinnamon, ginger, baking soda, and baking powder. Set aside. Beat butter, brown sugar, molasses, and egg. Beat mixture for 2 minutes. Add flour mixture alternately with milk. Beat well. Spread half of the batter in a greased 8x8x2-inch-baking dish. Pour cream cheese mixture over the batter in the dish. Top with remaining batter. Swirl cheese mixture and batter with a knife to create a marble effect. Bake at 350° for 45 minutes.

Cream Cheese Mixture:
2 (3 ounce) packages cream cheese, softened
3 tablespoons unbleached sugar
1 egg

Beat softened cream cheese, sugar, and egg. Beat 1 minute.

Gingerbread with Orange Sauce

1/2 cup butter
1/2 cup dark brown sugar
2 eggs
1/4 cup molasses
2/3 cup buttermilk
1 1/2 cups unbleached flour
1 teaspoon baking soda
1 teaspoon ginger
1 teaspoon cinnamon
1/2 teaspoon sea salt
1/2 teaspoon pepper

Cream butter and sugar together. Beat in eggs, molasses, and buttermilk. Combine flour, baking soda, ginger, cinnamon, salt, and pepper. Add to egg mixture and beat for 1 minute. Pour into an 8x8x2-inch greased baking dish. Bake at 325° for 45 minutes. Serve with orange sauce and whipped cream.

Orange Sauce:
Dissolve 2 tablespoons pure cornstarch with a little filtered water. Combine with 1 cup orange juice, 1 tablespoon grated orange peel, 6 tablespoons unbleached sugar, 1/2 teaspoon ginger and 1/2 teaspoon cinnamon. Cook over water or double boiler until thick. Whip cream with 2 tablespoons fructose.

Desserts

Candy/Treats/Fudge

Caramels

Caramel Corn

Peanut Brittle

Pecan Candy Roll

Pecan Pralines

Powdered Cereal

Fudge with Peanut Butter

Fudge Light and Dark

No Fail Fudge

Wet Walnuts

Caramels

2 cups unbleached or raw sugar
2 cups cream
1 3/4 cups corn syrup
1 cup butter
1 cup chopped nuts
Pinch of sea salt

Combine sugar, 1 cup cream, corn syrup, and butter. Boil 30 minutes. Add second cup of cream. Boil to firm ball stage (248° on candy thermometer). Add nuts and pour into a well-buttered pan. When cool cut into squares.

Caramel Corn

4 cups popped corn
1 cup brown sugar
1/2 teaspoon sea salt
1 stick butter
1/2 cup corn syrup
1/2 teaspoon baking soda

Combine sugar, salt, butter, and syrup. Cook on high for 2 minutes, stirring constantly. Stir in baking soda. Place popcorn in a large brown bag then pour syrup over the popcorn. Close bag and shake it. Microwave for 1 1/2 minutes. Shake. Microwave for 1 1/2 minutes. Shake. Microwaves vary in temperature. Adjust time accordingly. Dump out onto a cookie sheet to cool.

Variation: Sugar Coated Popcorn:
An easy way to fix corn without microwaving it is to use an automatic electric stirring popcorn popper. Place 1/4 cup oil in popper, heat, then add 1/2 cup brown or unbleached sugar, 1/2 teaspoon sea salt and 3/4 cup popcorn kernels. The popcorn is coated as it pops.

Peanut Brittle

1 cup unbleached sugar
1/2 cup corn syrup
1 tablespoon butter
1/8 teaspoon sea salt
1 cup peanuts, raw peanuts, or pecans
1/8 teaspoon pure vanilla
1/2 teaspoon baking soda

Caramelize sugar. To do so, cook sugar in a pan, stirring sugar until it is golden. Do not burn. Unbleached sugar may turn a little browner. That is okay. Stir in corn syrup and butter. Add salt, peanuts, and vanilla. Stir in baking soda. Stir only until blended. Pour a layer (about 1/4 inch) onto a well-buttered pan. When cool, cut or break peanut brittle into pieces.

Pecan Candy Roll

1 cup cream
2 cups unbleached sugar
1 cup brown sugar
1/2 cup corn syrup
1 1/2 cups chopped pecans

Boil cream, sugars, and syrup to soft-ball stage (235° on candy thermometer). Cool to room temperature. Beat until creamy. Turn onto a board, dusted with sugar or fructose. Knead until firm. Shape into a log and roll in fine chopped pecans until well coated. Place in refrigerator to cool. Slice with a sharp knife.

Pecan Pralines

1 cup light brown sugar
1 cup unbleached sugar
5 tablespoons filtered water
1 tablespoon butter
1/2 pound chopped pecans

Combine sugars, water, and butter. Cook and stir over medium heat. When mixture begins to boil rapidly, add pecans. Boil and stir constantly until mixture looks sugary. Remove from heat. Drop by spoonfuls onto a well buttered marble slab or a platter.

Variation: Combine 1 1/2 cups brown sugar, 1/2 cup unbleached sugar, and 1/2 cup evaporated milk in a saucepan. Boil and cook until a drop forms a soft ball in cold water (236°). Add 4 tablespoons butter and 2 cups chopped pecans and return to 236° stirring constantly. Remove from heat and add a teaspoon of pure vanilla. Beat until mixture begins to thicken. Drop by spoonfuls onto a waxed paper and let set to get firm. Top with a pecan half if desired.

Powdered Cereal

Powdered Cereal
(A healthy treat for kids)
1 stick butter
1 cup creamy peanut butter
12 ounces carob chips
1 large box pillow or waffle type cereal (all natural from a health food store)
1 pound homemade powdered sugar (Equal amounts of fructose & pure cornstarch)

Place butter, peanut butter, and carob chips in a saucepan and melt over water or in a double boiler. Place cereal in a large bowl and pour butter mixture over cereal. Mix until well coated. Place powdered sugar into a large paper bag with coated cereal and shake until coated. Open bag and let cool; shake occasionally. You may pour mixture onto a cookie sheet to cool.

Fudge with Peanut Butter

4 cups unbleached sugar
1 cup filtered water
2 egg whites
1 cup honey
1/2 cup peanut butter (all natural)
1 cup chopped peanuts
1 teaspoon pure vanilla

Boil 1 cup sugar and 1/2 cup water to soft-ball stage (236°). Beat egg whites until they are very stiff. Pour hot mixture over the egg whites. Beat constantly until mixture is stiff. Boil 3 cups sugar, honey, peanut butter and 1/2 cup water to soft ball stage (236°) degree. Slowly add to egg mixture. Beat continuously until mixture will hold its shape when dropped from a spoon. Add nuts and vanilla. Drop by spoonfuls onto waxed paper. Cool and serve.

Light and Dark Fudge

Dark Part:
3 cups unbleached sugar
1 1/2 tablespoons corn syrup
4 tablespoons carob or cocoa powder
1 1/2 cups cream
2 tablespoons butter
1 tablespoons pure vanilla

Combine sugar, syrup, cocoa, and cream. Boil to soft-ball stage (236°). Cool to room temperature. Add butter and vanilla. Beat until creamy. Pour into a well-buttered pan.

White Part:
3 cups unbleached sugar or fructose
1 1/2 tablespoons corn syrup
1 1/2 cups cream
2 tablespoons butter
1 tablespoons pure vanilla

Combine sugar, syrup, and cream. Boil to soft-ball stage (236°). Cool to room temperature. Add butter and vanilla. Pour over dark fudge mixture in same pan. Cool and cut into squares.

Hint: Add 1 teaspoon cornstarch to each cup sugar when making fudge. It will make the fudge creamier.

Hint: To keep fudge from boiling over rub butter around the top inside of the saucepan.

No Fail Fudge

2 cups unbleached sugar
2 tablespoons carob or cocoa powder
1 small can evaporated milk
1/2 package carob chips
1 tablespoons butter
1/2 cup nuts (optional)

Combine sugar, carob powder, and evaporated milk. Bring to rolling boil and cook for 2 minutes and 15 seconds. Remove from heat and add carob chips, butter, and vanilla. Add 1/2 cup chopped nuts if desired. Stir until carob chips are melted. Pour into a buttered pan. Cool and cut.

Wet Walnuts

Wet Walnuts
1 cup walnut pieces
1/4 cup pure maple syrup
1/4 cup light corn syrup

Heat nuts in frying pan over medium heat until heated through. Add syrup and cook until browned. Keep stirred to avoid burning. Cool on a buttered cookie sheet.

Desserts

Cookies

Apple Caramel Cookies

Banana Nut Cookies

Carob Chip Cookies

Carrot Oatmeal Cookies

Decorated Cookies

Double Carob Oatmeal Cookies

Gingerbread Cut Out Kids

Grandma's Soft Sugar Cookies

Honey Molasses Ginger Snaps

Molasses Cookies (soft)

Oatmeal Date Cookies

Orange Squash Cookies

Peanut Butter/Peanut Butter Cookies

Sour Cream Raisin Cookies

Apple Caramel Cookies

1 1/3 cup brown sugar
1/2 cup butter
1 egg
2 1/2 cups unbleached flour
2 teaspoons cinnamon
1 teaspoon baking soda
1/2 teaspoon sea salt
1/2 cup apple juice
3/4 cup grated apple
3/4 cup chopped walnut

Cream together butter and sugar. Add egg and beat. Combine flour, cinnamon, baking soda, and salt. Add to butter and egg mixture alternately with apple juice. Blend well and stir in grated apple and chopped nuts. Drop rounded spoonfuls onto greased baking sheet. Bake at 350° for 12 minutes. Cool and frost with caramel icing.

Caramel Icing:
Caramelize 1/2 cup unbleached sugar. Add 1/4 cup boiling, filtered water; stir until dissolved. Add 1/2 cup milk, 2 tablespoons butter, 1/8 teaspoon sea salt and 1 1/2 cups unbleached sugar. Boil to soft ball stage (236°). Cool. Stir in 1 teaspoon pure vanilla. Beat until thick and creamy. You may add homemade powdered sugar if icing is not thick enough to spread on cookies.

Banana Nut Cookies

3/4 cup softened butter
1 cup unbleached sugar
1 egg
1 3/4 cups mashed banana
1 1/2 cups unbleached flour
1/2 teaspoon baking soda
1 teaspoon sea salt
3/4 teaspoon cinnamon
1/2 teaspoon nutmeg
1/2 cup chopped walnuts
2 cups oatmeal

Cream butter and sugar together. Add egg and mashed banana. Combine flour, baking soda, salt, cinnamon, and 1/2 teaspoon nutmeg. Blend into the banana mixture. Mix well. Stir in chopped nuts and oatmeal. Chill in refrigerator for 2 hours. Drop by spoonfuls onto a greased cookie sheet. Bake at 350° for 12 minutes.

Suggestions: If you are in a hurry you can add another 1/2 cup of rolled oats to the dough and eliminate refrigerating.

Carob Chip Cookies

1 cup butter
1 cup lard or vegetable shortening
1 1/2 cups unbleached sugar
1 1/2 cups brown sugar
6 eggs
2 teaspoons pure vanilla
6 cups unbleached flour
2 teaspoons baking soda
1 teaspoon sea salt
1 cup chopped nuts
1 package carob chips

Cream butter, shortening, and sugars together. Add eggs and vanilla. Beat 1 minute. Combine flour, baking soda, and salt. Blend in with egg mixture. Stir in nuts and carob chips. Drop spoonfuls onto a greased cookie sheet. Bake at 375° for 10 minutes.

Carrot Oatmeal Cookies

1 stick softened butter
1/2 cup brown sugar
1 cup honey
2 eggs
1 cup unbleached flour
1 cup whole wheat flour
2 teaspoons baking powder
1/2 teaspoon baking soda
1/2 teaspoons sea salt
2 teaspoons cinnamon
1/2 teaspoon ginger
1/2 teaspoon nutmeg
4 cups cleaned and shredded carrots
2 cups rolled oats
2 cups chopped walnuts
1 cup raisins soaked in hot filtered water

Cream butter, sugar, and honey together. Add eggs and beat for 1 minute. Combine flours, baking powder, baking soda, sea salt, cinnamon, ginger, and nutmeg. Stir in egg and sugar mixture. Add carrots, oats, and nuts. Mix until well blended. Drain raisins and add to the batter. Mix and drop rounded tablespoons of cookie dough onto a foil covered cookie sheet. With floured hands flatten to 1/2 inch. Bake at 325° for 25 minutes.

Variation: Add 1/2 cup pecans to the batter.

Decorated Cookies

1 box dark brown sugar
1 cup lard
8 egg yolks
1/2 cup warm filtered water
1 teaspoon baking soda
1/2 teaspoon sea salt
1 teaspoon pure vanilla
4 1/2 cups unbleached flour

Cream sugar and lard together. Add egg yolks and beat for 1 minute. Blend in water, soda, salt and vanilla. Mix in flour. Chill overnight. Roll out dough and cut with cookie cutter. Dough should be thin. Bake at 350° for 10 minutes. Spread with cream cheese frosting or decorate with white frosting.

Cream Cheese Frosting:
Blend 3 ounce package of cream cheese, 1/4 cup milk, and enough homemade powdered sugar (equal parts of fructose and cornstarch) to make a frosting that will squeeze through a decorating tip. Divide frosting and tint with all natural food coloring.

White Frosting:
1 cup butter or vegetable shortening, 1/4 cup milk, 1 cup homemade powdered sugar. Blend. Add enough powdered sugar to make a soft frosting that will hold its shape through a decorator tip. Frost the cookies. Divide the remaining frosting and make several different colors.

Double Carob Oatmeal Cookies

These are very good
2 cups butter
2 cups unbleached sugar
2 cups brown sugar
4 eggs
1 tablespoon apple cider vinegar
2 teaspoons pure vanilla
4 cups unbleached flour
5 cups rolled oats (pulverize into a flour-like texture with a blender)
1 teaspoon sea salt
2 teaspoons baking powder
2 teaspoons baking soda
24 ounce package carob chips
8 ounce chunk of carob or chocolate, grated
2 cups chopped pecans

Cream butter and sugars together. Beat in eggs, vinegar, and vanilla. Combine flour, pulverized oatmeal, salt, baking powder, and baking soda. Add to egg mixture. Stir in carob chips, grated carob chunk, and chopped pecans. Roll into balls and place on a greased cookie sheet. Bake at 375° for 15 to 20 minutes. Baking time will depend on size of the cookie. If you prefer a soft cookie, add a piece of an apple and store in an airtight container. If you prefer a crisp cookie, store in a loose fitting container.

Gingerbread Cutout Kids

1 cup lard
1/2 cup unbleached sugar
1 egg
1 tablespoons apple cider vinegar
1/2 cup molasses
2 1/2 cups unbleached flour
1 teaspoon baking powder
1 teaspoon ground ginger
1/2 teaspoon baking soda
1 teaspoon cinnamon
1/2 teaspoon ground cloves
1/4 teaspoon cardamom

Cream lard and sugar until smooth. Blend in egg, vinegar, and molasses. Beat for 1 minute. Combine flour, baking powder, ginger, soda, cinnamon, cloves, and cardamom. Add 1 cup flour mixture to molasses mixture. Beat 1 minute. Stir in remaining flour mixture until well blended. Cover and chill overnight. Divide dough into 3 portions. Roll out on floured board to 1/4-inch thickness. Cut into desired size gingerbread kids. Place on a wax paper lined cookie sheet. Allow space between cookies so they do not bake into one another. Bake at 375° for 5 to 15 minutes, depending on the size of the cookies. Slide wax paper and cookies off the cookie sheet to cool. You may reuse the cookie sheet if necessary. Decorate with homemade powdered sugar frosting.

Homemade Powdered Sugar Frosting:
Combine 1/2 cup softened butter, 1 (3 ounces) package softened cream cheese, 1/2-cup milk, and 1 cup homemade powdered sugar. Beat for 1 minute. Add enough powdered sugar so icing can be consistently used in decorating.

Hint: Dip cookie cutter in oil before cutting.

Homemade Powdered Sugar: Use equal parts Sorbitol or fructose and pure cornstarch.

Grandma's Soft Sugar Cookies

1 cup softened lard
1 cup unbleached sugar
1 cup brown sugar
3 eggs
4 cups unbleached flour
1 teaspoon baking soda
2 teaspoons baking powder
1 teaspoon nutmeg
1/2 teaspoon sea salt
1 cup milk

Cream lard and sugars together. Beat in eggs. Combine flour, baking soda, baking powder, nutmeg, and salt. Add to egg mixture alternately with milk. Chill overnight. Roll out on floured board. Cut with a large 4-inch cookie cutter. Place on a greased cookie sheet. Sprinkle with unbleached sugar. Bake at 350° until done. Do not overbake. Test by pressing a finger into the cookie. When done the cookie should spring back.

Suggestion: Dip cookie cutter in oil before cutting.

Honey Molasses Ginger Snaps

1/3 cup brown sugar
1/4 cup honey
1/4 cup molasses
1/4 cup softened butter
1 egg
1 teaspoon apple cider vinegar
2 cups unbleached flour
3/4 teaspoon ginger
1/2 teaspoon cinnamon
1/4 teaspoon nutmeg
1/4 teaspoon allspice
1/8 teaspoon cloves
Pinch of pepper
1/4 teaspoon sea salt
1/2 teaspoon baking soda

Blend together sugar, honey, molasses, butter, egg, and vinegar. Cook over low heat until mixture boils, stirring occasionally. Cool to room temperature. Combine flour, ginger, cinnamon, nutmeg, allspice, cloves, pepper, salt, and soda. Add to cooled molasses mixture. Mix with hands until dough is smooth and elastic. Cover and refrigerate overnight. Divide dough into three portions. Roll out on floured board 1/8-inch thick. Sprinkle dough with raw sugar. With rolling pin lightly press sugar into the dough. Cut into desired shapes. Place on greased cookie sheets. Bake at 350° for 10 minutes.

Hint: Keep sugar in a shaker then just shake the sugar on to the cookies.

Hint: To crisp up cookies place in a 300° oven for 5 minutes.

Suggestion: Make ginger snap sandwiches. Cut round cookies and bake. Place a teaspoon of raspberry jam between two cookies.

Molasses Cookies (Soft)

1/2 cup lard
1/4 cup butter
1 cup brown sugar, packed
1 egg
1/4 cup molasses
2 cups unbleached flour
2 teaspoons baking soda
2 teaspoons cinnamon
1 1/2 teaspoons ginger
1 teaspoon ground cloves
1/2 teaspoon nutmeg
1 teaspoon sea salt

Cream softened lard, softened butter, and sugar. Add egg and molasses. Beat for 1 minute. Combine flour, baking soda, cinnamon, ginger, cloves, nutmeg, and salt. Chill overnight. Shape into balls. Dip balls into ice water and then raw sugar. Place on cookie sheet. Bake at 350° for 10 minutes.

Suggestion: To make a softer cookie, add 1 teaspoon jelly to butter first.

Hint: Lard makes cookies softer.

Oatmeal Date Cookies

1 1/2 cups melted lard
2 cups brown sugar
4 eggs
6 tablespoons milk
2 teaspoons pure vanilla
4 cups unbleached flour
1 1/2 teaspoons baking soda
2 teaspoons sea salt
4 cups rolled oats
3 cups dates or raisins
1 1/2 cups chopped nuts

Cream lard and sugar together. Add eggs, milk, and vanilla. Beat for 1 minute. Combine flour, baking soda, and salt. Blend in with egg mixture. Grind together rolled oats and dates or raisins. Add to batter. Stir in chopped nuts. Drop by spoonfuls onto a greased cookie sheet. Bake at 375° for 12 minutes.

Hint: Place hardened brown sugar in the microwave with a piece of apple and microwave for a few minutes to soften.

Orange Squash Cookies

1 cup softened butter
1/2 cup brown sugar
1 egg
1 3/4 cups cooked squash
2 tablespoons orange juice
2 1/2 cups unbleached flour
1/2 teaspoon baking soda
1/2 teaspoon sea salt
1 teaspoon grated orange peel
1/2 cup chopped walnuts

Cream butter and sugar together. Blend in egg, squash, and orange juice. Combine flour, baking soda, salt, and orange peel. Add 1 cup flour mixture to egg mixture and beat for 1 minute. Add remaining flour and mix until well blended. Stir in nuts. Drop by spoonfuls onto a lightly greased cookie sheet. Bake at 375° for 12 minutes. Frost cooled cookie with orange frosting.

Orange Frosting:
Blend 1/4 cup orange juice, 1 teaspoon grated orange peel. Heat slightly and add enough homemade powdered sugar to make it spreadable. Cool. Frost cookies.

Peanut Butter/Peanut Butter Cookies

4 1/2 cups unbleached flour
1 1/2 cups unbleached sugar
1 1/2 teaspoon baking soda
3/4 teaspoon sea salt
1 1/2 cups softened lard
1 1/2 cups peanut butter
3 tablespoons milk
3/4 cup corn syrup
Peanut butter for filling

Combine flour, sugar, baking soda, and salt. Blend in lard and peanut butter. Stir in milk and syrup. Shape into two logs and chill over night. Make slices 1/4 inch thick and spread with 1/2 teaspoon peanut butter, cover with second slice. Seal by pressing the edges with a fork. Bake on greased cookie sheet at 375° for 10 minutes.

Comment: You can make your own peanut butter by processing peanuts in a blender. Add unbleached sugar or fructose to peanuts. If it seems too dry add a little peanut oil.

Sour Cream Raisin Cookies

2 cups light brown sugar
1/2 cup melted lard
2 eggs
1 cup sour cream
3 cups unbleached flour
1/2 teaspoon cinnamon
1/2 teaspoon nutmeg
1 teaspoon sea salt
1/2 teaspoon baking soda
1 teaspoon baking powder
1 cup chopped raisins
1/2 cup chopped nuts

Beat sugar, lard, eggs, and sour cream. Combine flour, cinnamon, nutmeg, salt, baking soda, and baking powder. Add to the egg mixture. Mix well. Stir in raisins and nuts. Drop by spoonfuls onto a greased cookie sheet. Bake at 425° for 10 minutes.

Optional: Vanilla Glaze
Mix 2 tablespoons milk, 1 teaspoon pure vanilla, and enough homemade powdered sugar to make a drizzly frosting. Drizzle over cooled cookies.

Desserts

Frosting/Icing

Boiled Brown Sugar Frosting

Boiled Frosting

Coffee Frosting

German Carob Frosting

Fudge Frosting

Creamy Maple Butter Frosting

Orange Cream Cheese Frosting

Baker's Icing

Lemon Butter Icing

Vinegar Icing

Boiled Brown Sugar Frosting

1 cup brown sugar
1/4 teaspoon sea salt
1/4 teaspoon cream of tartar
1 egg white
1/3 cup boiling filtered water

Combine all ingredients. Cook in double boiler. While cooking, beat until mixture forms stiff peaks.

Boiled Frosting

1 cup fructose
1/3 cup filtered water
2 egg whites
1/2 teaspoon cream of tartar
1 teaspoon pure vanilla

Cook fructose and water until a 6-inch thread spins when spilled from a spoon. Beat egg whites and cream of tartar until stiff peaks form. Blend in vanilla. Great on angel cake.

Cherry Frosting: Use cherry juice in place of water.

Lemon Frosting: Use pure lemon extract in place of vanilla.

Pineapple: Use 1/2 cup cooked, sweetened crushed, pineapple, well drained. Add 1 teaspoon lemon rind. Omit the vanilla.

Strawberry Frosting: Add fresh strawberries to frosting.

Coffee Frosting

2 egg whites
1 cup unbleached sugar
1/4 cup filtered water
1 tablespoon instant espresso (from health food store)

Combine all ingredients and cook over water. While cooking, beat with an electric mixer on high speed for 7 minutes. Beat until thick and cool.

German Carob Frosting

1 cup condensed milk
1 cup unbleached sugar
3 egg yolks
1 stick butter
1 teaspoon pure vanilla
1 1/2 cups shredded coconut
1 cup chopped pecans

Boil milk, sugar, egg yolks, butter, and vanilla in a double boiler about 2 minutes. Add coconut and pecans. Cool and frost carob cake.

Fudge Frosting

2 squares unsweetened chocolate
1 1/2 cups unbleached sugar
1/4 cup butter
1/4 teaspoon sea salt
7 tablespoons milk
1 tablespoon corn syrup
1 teaspoon pure vanilla

In a saucepan combine all ingredients except vanilla. Bring to boil. Cook over low heat 2 minutes (230°). Cool to lukewarm. Add vanilla. Beat until frosting is thick enough to spread. If too thick add cream. Spread on chocolate or carob cake and sprinkle with nuts.

Suggestion: Add a pinch of baking soda to frosting.

Creamy Maple Butter Frosting

8 egg yolks
2 cup pure maple syrup
2 cups butter
1 teaspoon pure vanilla
1/4 cup homemade powdered sugar

Beat egg yolks, for 3 minutes. Heat maple syrup to boiling point. Cook to 240° on the candy thermometer (soft-ball stage), approximately 10 to 15 minutes. Remove from heat. With an electric mixer, slowly pour a stream of syrup onto the edge of the bowl and mix into the yolks. Be sure the syrup touches the edge of the bowl. Continue beating until syrup and egg are well incorporated. This should take approximately 5 minutes. Mix until slightly warm. Add butter and mix 5 additional minutes or until fluffy. Stir in homemade powdered sugar as needed.

Orange Cream Cheese Frosting

¾ cup softened butter
3 (8 ounce) packages cream cheese, softened
1 tablespoon grated orange rind
2 tablespoons fresh grated ginger
Pinch of sea salt
Homemade powdered sugar

Combine butter, cream cheese, orange rind, ginger, and salt. Add enough powdered sugar to make a spreadable frosting. Beat until fluffy, about 3 minutes.

Baker's Icing

1 cup milk
4 tablespoons unbleached flour
1 cup softened butter
Pinch of sea salt
1 cup unbleached sugar
1 teaspoon pure vanilla

Mix milk and flour in a saucepan. Cook until smooth and thick. Cool. Add butter and blend at low speed. Add salt and sugar and beat at high speed until fluffy and all crystals are dissolved. Add vanilla and beat 1 minute at high speed.

Variation: For chocolate or carob, add 6 tablespoons cocoa or carob powder dissolved in 2 tablespoons hot milk. Add to mixture and beat.

Food coloring:
Blue: Use blueberry juice.
Red: Use cranberry juice.
Yellow: Use lemon juice, butter and lemon extract.
Green: Use butter, lemon juice or extract and blueberry juice.

Lemon Butter Icing

3 ounces cream cheese
2 tablespoons cream
1/2 cup softened butter
3 teaspoons grated lemon rind
1 teaspoon pure lemon extract
2 cups homemade powdered sugar

Cream together cream cheese, cream, butter, lemon rind, and lemon extract. Add enough homemade powdered sugar to make a spreadable frosting and beat until fluffy.

Vinegar Icing

1 cup brown sugar
1 cup unbleached sugar
2/3 cup filtered water
1/8 teaspoon cream of tartar
2 egg whites
1 teaspoon pure vanilla
2 tablespoons apple cider vinegar

Combine brown sugar, sugar, water, and cream of tartar. Cook to soft-ball stage (236°). Pour slowly, beating constantly, onto stiffly beaten egg whites. Add vanilla and vinegar. Beat 1 minute.

Desserts

Fried Cakes/Donuts, Yeast Dough/Pastry/Crescents

Drizzle Cake

Drop Applesauce Donuts

Pumpkin Donuts

Raised Sugar Donuts

Apple Dividing Bread

Buchta with Nut Filling

Butter Horn Rolls

Prague Kolache

Sweet Roll Dough (Cinnamon Rolls)

Crescents

Rolachi (Nut Crescent)

Drizzle Cake

1/4 cup unbleached sugar
2 cups unbleached flour
1 1/2 teaspoons baking powder
1/4 teaspoon sea salt
2 eggs
1 1/2 cups milk
Peanut oil to fry in
Homemade powdered sugar

Combine sugar, flour, baking powder, and salt. Beat eggs, stir in milk and add to the flour mixture. Heat oil to 375°. Drizzle 1/2 cup batter into the hot oil in a circular motion. Fry 2 minutes or until light brown. Turn once. Drain on paper towel. Sprinkle with homemade powdered sugar or cinnamon and unbleached sugar.

Cinnamon and sugar mixture: Combine 1 cup unbleached sugar and 2 teaspoons cinnamon.

Homemade powdered sugar: Mix equal amounts of pure cornstarch and fructose or sorbitol.

Drop Applesauce Donuts

3 tablespoons butter
3/4 cup unbleached sugar
3 eggs
1 cup applesauce
1 teaspoon pure vanilla
4 1/2 cups unbleached flour
3 1/2 teaspoons baking powder
1 teaspoon sea salt
1/2 teaspoon cinnamon
1/4 teaspoon nutmeg
1/4 cup milk
Peanut or canola oil
Additional sugar for coating

Cream butter and sugar together. Add eggs, applesauce, and vanilla. Combine flour, baking powder, salt, cinnamon, and nutmeg. Add to butter and sugar mixture alternately with milk. This will make a thick batter. Heat oil to 375° in deep skillet or deep fryer. Drop by spoonfuls into the hot oil. Fry 1 minute on each side or until golden. Drizzle warm donuts with orange glaze and serve.

Orange Glaze:
Heat 2 cups homemade powdered sugar (equal parts fructose and pure cornstarch), 3 tablespoons orange juice and 1 teaspoon orange peel.

Comment: Peanut oil will give donuts a special flavor.

Pumpkin Donuts

2 eggs
1 cup unbleached sugar
2 tablespoons butter
1 cup prepared pumpkin
1 tablespoons lemon juice
4 1/2 cups unbleached flour
1 teaspoons baking powder
1 teaspoon baking soda
1/2 teaspoon sea salt
1/2 teaspoon cinnamon
1/2 teaspoon nutmeg
1 cup cream or evaporated milk
Peanut or canola oil

Cream eggs, sugar, and butter together. Add pumpkin and lemon juice. Combine flour, baking powder, baking soda, salt, cinnamon, and nutmeg. Add pumpkin mixture alternately with milk. Cover and refrigerate for 2 hours. Turn onto floured board and knead for 5 minutes. Roll out 1/2-inch thick. Cut with donut cutter. Fry in hot oil at 375°, 1 1/2 minutes each side or until golden. Frost.

Frosting:
Stir 3 tablespoons orange juice, 1 tablespoon evaporated milk or cream and 1 teaspoon grated orange rind into 2 cups homemade powdered sugar. Add sugar or cream for the consistency you want.

Raised Sugar Donuts

1 1/4 cups milk
1/4 cup unbleached sugar
1 teaspoon sea salt
1 package yeast
1/4 cup butter
2 egg yolks
3 1/2 cups unbleached flour
Peanut or canola oil for frying

Scald milk. Cool. Add sugar, salt, and yeast. Let stand 5 minutes. Add melted butter and egg yolks. Gradually add flour working it in until dough is smooth. Cover and let rise to double. Turn onto a floured board. Roll out 1/2-inch thick and cut with a donut cutter. Let rise to double. Fry in hot oil at 360° for 3 minutes or until golden. Turning once. When cool, shake donuts in a bag with cinnamon and sugar or glaze.

Glaze:
Cook 1/4 cup filtered water, 1 cup unbleached sugar or fructose, and vanilla.

Donut Hole Surprise:
Grease muffin tins or line with paper cupcake holders. Place 1 teaspoon brown sugar in each cup along with 1 teaspoon corn syrup, 1/2 teaspoon filtered water, 1 tablespoon chopped nuts and 4 raisins. Arrange 4 uncooked donut holes on top of syrup mixture. Cover and let rise until double. Bake at 350° for 25 minutes.

Apple Dividing Bread

1 package yeast
1 cup warm milk
2 tablespoons unbleached sugar
2 tablespoons butter
1 egg
1 teaspoon sea salt
3 1/2 cups unbleached flour
1 stick melted butter for dipping dough
Mixture to fill in between:
1 apple, peeled and chopped
1/2 teaspoon cinnamon
1/2 cup chopped pecans

Dissolve yeast in warm milk with 2 tablespoons sugar. Combine butter, egg, salt, and 2 cups flour. Beat until smooth. Add yeast mixture and remaining flour. Knead until dough is elastic. Place in a greased bowl, cover, and let rise to double in size. Punch down and cut in half. Cut each half in 16 pieces. Roll out each piece to a 2 1/2 inch circle.

Combine apple, cinnamon, and pecans. Divide in half and set aside. Place 1 teaspoon pecan mixture in each circle. Close and pinch together forming a ball. Dip each ball into melted butter. Place 16 balls in a 10-inch tube pan and sprinkle with remaining pecan mixture. Repeat process for remaining 16 balls. Place remaining 16 balls on top and sprinkle with remaining pecan mixture. Cover and let rise to double, about 1 hour. Bake at 350° for 40 minutes. Remove from pan and pull apart to serve.

Buchta with Nut Filling

1/2 cup milk
1/2 pound melted butter
2 tablespoons unbleached sugar
1 package yeast
5 egg yolks
4 cups unbleached flour

Heat milk. Add butter and sugar. Cool to lukewarm and add yeast. Let stand for 5 minutes. Beat egg yolks. Add to milk mixture and stir into flour. Mix well and form into 4 balls. Refrigerate overnight. The next day allow dough to warm and rise to double its size. Roll out on floured board. Spread with nut filling. Roll up like a jellyroll. Cover and let rise for 3 hours or until double. Bake at 350° for 45 minutes. Frost or glaze if desired.

Nut Filling:
Beat 12 egg whites until frothy. Add 1 pound homemade powdered sugar (equal parts fructose or sorbitol and pure cornstarch), and 2 pounds ground walnuts.

Frosting or Glaze:
Mix 2 cups homemade powdered sugar, 1 teaspoon pure vanilla, and enough milk to make a spreadable frosting or glaze.

Variation: Poppy Seed Filling:
Scald 1 1/2 cups milk, add 1/4 cup butter, pour scalding milk over 1 pound ground poppy seeds. Mix well with 3 cups unbleached sugar. Stir in 1 tablespoon pure vanilla. Cool overnight and spread on dough.

Butter Horn Rolls

1 package yeast
1 cup scalded milk
1 1/4 teaspoon sea salt
3 eggs, well beaten
1/2 cup lard
1/4 cup unbleached sugar
4 1/2 cup unbleached flour

Dissolve yeast in lukewarm milk, let stand for 5 minutes. Add salt, eggs, lard, and sugar. Add flour a little at a time until dough is stiff enough to knead on a floured board. Knead until dough is smooth and elastic. Cover with a damp cloth and let rise to double in size. Work down and let dough rise again. Turn out on floured board; shape into balls or crescents. Place on a greased cookie sheet and let dough rise to triple in size. Bake at 450° for 12 minutes. Bake until rolls are light tan. Brush with melted butter. For whole-wheat rolls, substitute half of the white flour with whole-wheat flour. Add 3 teaspoons gluten.

Hint: When using whole grain flour it is best to use gluten to help the rising process. Add 1 to 1 1/2 teaspoons gluten, for each cup whole grain flour.

Prague Kolache

1 package yeast
1 tablespoons warm filtered water
6 egg yolks
4 tablespoons unbleached sugar
1 pint cream
4 cups unbleached flour
1/2 teaspoon nutmeg
1/2 pound butter, softened
Pinch sea salt

Dissolve yeast in warm water. Let set to bubble. Beat egg yolks, sugar, and cream. Stir in 2 cups flour with yeast mixture, nutmeg, butter and salt. Blend in remaining flour and mix until dough is smooth and elastic. Let rise in the bowl until dough is double in size. Make balls the size of an egg and make an indentation; fill with prune, poppy seed (from buchta recipes), or cottage cheese filling. Close and pinch together. Place on greased cookie sheet ensuring closure is on the bottom. Make another indentation in the top of the kolache. Brush top of kolache with egg white. Using your fingers take a pinch of the streusel topping and push into the dent. Let rise to double. Bake at 400° for 15 minutes or until light brown. Serve with a dusting of homemade powdered sugar.

Cottage Cheese Filling:
Mix together 2 pounds dry cottage cheese, 3 egg yolks, 1/2 cup melted butter, 1 cup unbleached sugar or fructose, 1/2 cup raisins and 1/2 cup sweet cream.

Prune Filling:
Combine 2 eggs, 1 cup unbleached sugar, 1 cup cooked, chopped prunes, 1/2 cup sour cream, 2 tablespoons melted butter and 1/8 teaspoon sea salt. Place in a saucepan with a little filtered water and cook and stir until spreadable. Stir in 1 teaspoon pure vanilla.

Streusel Topping: Mix 1 cup unbleached flour, 1 cup unbleached sugar and 9 tablespoons softened butter. Mix until crumbly.

Sweet Roll Dough
(Cinnamon Rolls)

2 packages yeast
1/2 cup warm filtered water
1 1/2 cups lukewarm milk
1/2 cup lard, softened
1/2 cup unbleached sugar
2 teaspoons sea salt
2 eggs
5 cups unbleached flour

Filling:
Cinnamon
unbleached sugar
butter
raisins

Dissolve yeast in warm water. Add to lukewarm milk. Cream lard, sugar, salt, and eggs. Add to yeast and milk mixture. Stir part of the flour into the mixture and beat well. Add remaining flour and knead using the least amount of flour. This will make softer cinnamon rolls. Let dough rise to double in size. Punch down. Let it rise again. Turn half of the dough on a floured board. Roll out to 1/2-inch thick. Sprinkle with sugar and cinnamon. Dab with butter and a handful of fresh raisins, you may add more if you like. Roll up and cut into 1-inch thick slices and place in a greased baking dish. Let rise to double in size. Bake at 375° for 12 minutes. Frost with white frosting.

White Frosting:
Combine 1 stick softened butter, 2 cups homemade powdered sugar, and a little milk to make a spreadable frosting.

Apricot Crescents

1 cup butter
2 cups unbleached flour
1 egg
1/2 cup sour cream
1/2 cup homemade apricot preserves
1/2 cup shredded coconut
1/4 cup chopped pecans

Cut butter into flour. Combine egg yolk and sour cream. Stir into flour mixture and form into a ball. Divide dough into balls the size of an egg and chill for 4 hours. Roll out each ball into a 10 inch circle. Spread apricot preserves on each circle, sprinkle with 2 Tablespoons coconut and 1 Tablespoon pecans. Cut each circle into 12 wedges. Roll each wedge beginning at the wide end and rolling toward the small end. Brush each crescent with egg white or milk and sprinkle with unbleached sugar. Place on a cookie sheet, point side down, and bake at 350° for 22 minutes.

Apricot Preserves:
Soak 3 tablespoons finely chopped apricots in filtered boiling water. Let stand for 5 minutes. Drain. Combine 1/2 cup butter, 2 teaspoons unbleached sugar, 1 1/2 teaspoons grated ginger, and 1/2 teaspoon ground ginger. Beat until spreadable.

Rolachi
(Nut Crescent)

1 cup cream
12 egg yolks
4 cups unbleached flour
1 pound butter, softened
Filling:
2 pounds ground walnuts
12 egg whites
1 pound homemade powdered sugar

Stir cream and egg yolks. Combine flour and butter. Blend in egg mixture. Knead on floured board for 5 minutes. Form dough into balls the size of an egg. Flatten and place in container with wax paper between layers. Chill overnight. Take one or two pieces out, keeping others in refrigerator. Roll out in a very thin circle. Cut in 4 pieces (like pie wedges) and fill with nut mixture. Roll up starting at the wide end and rolling to the narrow end, forming a crescent with the point down. Place on cookie sheet and let rest 15 minutes before baking. Bake at 350° until dough springs back when pressed. Bottom should be tan but top should be very light. Serve with a sprinkle of homemade powdered sugar (equal parts sorbitol or fructose and pure cornstarch).

Nut Filling:
Grind 2 pounds walnut meat and add to 12 egg whites that have been beaten to a froth. Stir in 1 pound powdered sugar (homemade).

Hint: Do not substitute oleo for butter nor milk for cream. The crescent will be hard not light and flaky.

Desserts

Frozen Desserts/Ice Cream/Toppings

Blueberry Frozen Dessert

¼ cup unbleached sugar
½ envelope unflavored gelatin (1½ teaspoons)
1½ cups filtered water
1½ cup fresh blueberries
3 tablespoons lemon juice

Combine sugar, gelatin, and 1 cup water in a sauce pan. Heat until dissolved. Remove from heat. Add remaining water, berries, and lemon juice. Freeze until almost frozen, but able to mix in blender or mixer at low speed for 2 minutes. Return to freezer.

Honey Ice Cream

2 quarts half and half
1½ cups honey
2 tablespoons pure vanilla
½ teaspoon sea salt

Combine all ingredients and place in electric freezer and freeze according to directions.

Suggestion: This can also be made in refrigerator freezers. Stir occasionally until frozen.

Vanilla Ice Cream

12 eggs
1 gallon milk
6 cups unbleached sugar or fructose
4 tablespoons unbleached flour or pure cornstarch
2 tablespoons sea salt
1 quart of cream
4 to 6 tablespoons pure vanilla (to taste)

Blend eggs, milk, sugar, flour, and salt. Cook over water or in a double boiler just to the boiling point. Chill until cold. Add cream and vanilla. Place in freezer container. Put crushed ice around container in freezer. Add 2 1/2 cups rock salt. Churn until it sounds like it is turning hard. Remove paddle from ice cream. Replace and secure cover. Pack with ice until ready to serve. This may be frozen in freezer.

Suggestion: Coffee Ice Cream: add 1/4 cup instant coffee (from health food store).

Suggestion: Smaller recipe:
6 cups milk
2 cups half and half
6 eggs
3 cups milk
3 tablespoons unbleached flour or cornstarch
3 cups fructose
1/4 teaspoon sea salt
2 tablespoons pure vanilla
2 cups cream

Lemon Ice Cream

3 cups milk
2 cups fructose
4 egg yolks
2 eggs
1 cup cream
2 cups half and half
3/4 cup lemon juice
1 tablespoons lemon rind
1 teaspoon sea salt
2 tablespoons pure vanilla

Combine milk, fructose, yolks, and eggs. Cook over water or double boiler just to boiling point. Cool. Add cream, half and half, juice, rind, salt, and vanilla. Freeze in ice cream freezer or in refrigerator freezer.

Variations:
Add fruit to ice cream;
a little apple cider vinegar;
add pure peppermint flavoring;
add 1 2/3 cups shredded carob, before ice cream is solid;
add 2 cups orange juice (in place of lemon juice and 1 1/4 cups milk) and grated rind from 2 oranges;
add 1 cup lime juice in place of lemon juice and 1/4 cup milk.

Muddy River Pie

1 stick butter
2 pounds homemade chocolate cookie crumbs
1/2 gallon homemade coffee ice cream
3 cups homemade hot fudge
1 cup chopped pecans

Melt butter and stir in cookie crumbs. Divide between two pie plates that have been buttered. Divide softened ice cream between the crusts. Freeze for 12 hours. Cover with hot fudge topping and sprinkle with chopped pecans.

Comment: Drizzle with caramel if you dare.

Butterscotch Sauce

3/4 cup unbleached sugar
1/2 cup corn syrup
1/4 teaspoon sea salt
1/4 cup butter
1 cup cream
1 teaspoon pure vanilla

Combine sugar, syrup, salt, butter, and 1/2 cup cream. Cook over medium low heat to soft-ball stage (236°). Stir in the other 1/2 cup cream and cook to thick consistency (228°). Remove from heat and stir in vanilla.

Caramel Sauce

1 1/2 cups unbleached sugar
1 1/2 cups brown sugar
1 heaping tablespoon unbleached flour
2 tablespoons corn syrup
1 tablespoons cream

Mix all ingredients. Boil slowly until it reaches soft-ball stage (236°). Remove from heat but do not stir. If mixture sugars add more cream and reheat.

Choclate Syrup

2 cups unbleached sugar
1 cup cocoa or carob powder
1/4 teaspoon sea salt
1 cup filtered water

Combine all ingredients and simmer for 5 minutes.

Hot Fudge Sauce

1/2 cup butter
3 (1 ounce) unsweetened chocolate squares
1 (12 ounce) can evaporated milk
2 to 4 cups homemade powdered sugar

Melt butter and chocolate. Add milk. Beat in 2 cups powdered sugar. Gradually add more powdered sugar until you have reached the desired consistency.

Desserts

Fruit Salads

Apple Salad

Creamed Fruit Salad

Fruit Salad Dressing

Fruit and Sour Cream Dressing

Fruit Dessert

Orange Gelatin

Orange Salad

Pineapple Gelatin Dessert

Mixed Fruit with Orange Poppy Seed Dressing

Apple Salad

4 cups apples, peeled and cored
1/2 cup filtered water
1/2 cup unbleached sugar
Cinnamon or nutmeg
1/4 cup raisins
1/4 cup chopped pecans or walnuts

Slice apples. Combine apples and add water. Cover and cook until soft. Do not drain water. Beat apples until smooth. Add sugar and cinnamon or nutmeg to taste. Add raisins. Cover and simmer until sugar is dissolved. Stir in nuts.

Comment: Apples are sprayed so be sure to wash them thoroughly before eating them. Use water with a little apple cider vinegar.

Suggestion: Save apple peel and cook to make apple juice or jelly.

Creamed Fruit Salad

2 cans mixed fruit (canned in its own juice)
1 cup whipping cream
8 ounces cream cheese

Drain fruit. Whip cream and mix with softened cream cheese. Stir in fruit. Chill and serve.

Help Hint: If using fresh fruit, add a pinch of sea salt to the cream before adding the fruit. This will help to keep it from curdling.

Fruit Salad Dressing

2 tablespoons pure cornstarch
1 cup unbleached sugar
1/4 cup honey
2 cups unsweetened pineapple juice
2 cups unsweetened orange juice
1/4 cup lemon juice

Combine all ingredients and cook for 3 minutes. Stir while cooking. Cool and pour over fruit mixture of your choice.

Help Hint: Soak oranges in hot water before squeezing to yield more juice.

Fruit and Sour Cream Dressing

1 cup sour cream
3 tablespoons unbleached sugar
1/2 teaspoon sea salt
Juice from 1/2 lemon
1 teaspoon apple cider vinegar

Mix well and use over fruit or vegetable combination.

Fruit Dessert

1 envelope unflavored gelatin
1/3 cup fructose
1/8 teaspoon sea salt
1 3/4 cups any natural all fruit juice (bottled 100% real fruit juice may be substituted)
1/2 teaspoon grated lemon rind

Mix gelatin, fructose, and salt. Add 1/2 cup juice. Cook and stir over low heat until dissolved. Remove from heat. Stir in remaining juice and rind. Chill until mixture begins to thicken. Beat with mixer until fluffy. Place in individual dessert dishes. Chill until firm.

Suggestion: When recipe calls for grated lemon rind, grate the whole rind. Dry and save the remaining rind in a jar for later.

Orange Gelatin

1 tablespoon unflavored gelatin
1/2 cup cold filtered water
3/4 cup boiling filtered water
1/3 cup fructose
Pinch sea salt
2 tablespoons lemon juice
1/2 cup orange juice

Soften gelatin in cold water. Dissolve in boiling water. Add fructose and salt. Stir until dissolved. Add strained fruit juices. Pour into mold and chill.

Variation: Try other fruit juices. If you prefer more flavor, add more fruit juice and cut down on the amount of water.

Orange Salad

1 envelope unflavored gelatin
2 tablespoons fructose
1/4 teaspoon sea salt
1/2 cup cold filtered water
3/4 cup filtered water
1/2 cup orange juice
1 tablespoon lemon juice
1 tablespoons apple cider vinegar
1 orange, peeled, sectioned, and diced
1 cup fine, shredded and chopped cabbage
1/4 cup celery finely chopped

In a saucepan mix gelatin, fructose, salt, and 1/2 cup cold water. Cook and stir over low heat until gelatin and fructose are dissolved. Stir in 3/4 cup water, orange juice, lemon juice, and vinegar. Chill until partially set. Fold in remaining ingredients. If desired, pour into a mold. Chill until firm.

Pineapple Gelatin Dessert

1 cup fresh crushed pineapple cooked in 1/2 cup filtered water and 1/2 cup fructose
1 envelope unflavored gelatin
1/4 cup orange juice
1/4 cup fructose
1/4 teaspoon sea salt
3/4 cup pineapple syrup
1/2 cup black cherries, cut in half and seeded
1/2 cup shredded carrots

Prepare pineapple. Drain juice. Dissolve gelatin in 1/4 cup orange juice. Add fructose, salt, 3/4 cup syrup from pineapple, cherries, and carrots. Mix together and chill until firm.

Help Hint: Always cook fresh pineapple with unbleached sugar or fructose when making a gelatin. If you use fresh pineapple without cooking it before hand, the gelatin will not set up.

Mixed Fruit with Orange Poppyseed Dressing

1/4 cup orange juice
3 tablespoons apple cider vinegar
2 tablespoons mustard
3 tablespoons honey
1 tablespoon Worcestershire sauce
1 teaspoon grated orange rind
1/2 teaspoon sea salt
1/2 cup canola oil
1 tablespoons poppy seeds
6 cups fruit: any combination of cantaloupe, watermelon, honeydew melon, blueberries, blackberries, grapes, star fruit, strawberries, or nectarines.

Combine all ingredients except fruit and poppy seeds. Mix 6 cups any combination of fruit in a large bowl. Stir poppy seeds in the dressing and pour over the fruit. If desired, serve on a bed of lettuce.

Desserts

Pies

Apple Pie

Apple Pie with Sour Cream

Blueberry Pie with Pineapple

Cottage Pie

Fruit Medley Pie

Nectarine Cherry Pie

Peach Pie

Strawberry Pie

Basic Vanilla Pie Filling, Cooked Meringue

Cream Pie (Banana), (Carob or Chocolate), (Coconut), (Pineapple), (Raisin)

Custard Pie

Lemon Meringue Pie

Pecan Pie

Pumpkin Pie

Apple Pie

6 cups apples
1/2 cup unbleached sugar
1/2 cup brown sugar
3/4 teaspoon cinnamon
1/8 teaspoon allspice
1/4 cup unbleached flour
1/8 teaspoon sea salt
1 tablespoon lemon juice
2 tablespoons butter

Peel and core apples and place in salt water to keep them from turning brown. Drain. Place sliced apples in a bowl with sugars, cinnamon, allspice, flour, salt, and juice. Stir until mixture becomes moist. Pour into an unbaked pie shell and dab with butter. Cover with a layer of pie dough, flute, and seal edges. Moisten top crust with melted butter or beaten egg white. Sprinkle with raw sugar and bake at 375° for 1 1/2 hours or until crust is tanned and a knife inserted shows apples are cooked. I recommend using My Favorite Pie Crust recipe located with Peach Pie recipe.

Suggestion: Slit holes in top crust to keep pie from running over.

Suggestion: Keep sugar in shaker to sprinkle on pie.

Suggestion: You may purchase a pie drip pan that will hold the pie above the run over if it should occur.

Suggestion: Sprinkle about 1/2 cup oatmeal in the bottom of a pastry lined pie plate before adding the apple mixture to help keep the mixture from running over.

Hint: Keep in mind that all ovens vary so food should be checked often.

Apple Pie with Sour Cream

2 pounds apples
2 tablespoons lemon juice
1 (8 ounce) container sour cream
3/4 cup unbleached sugar
2 tablespoons unbleached flour
1 teaspoon pure vanilla
1/8 teaspoon sea salt
1 egg
1 teaspoon cinnamon

Peel and slice apples. Place in salt water until all are peeled. Drain. Place in bowl with lemon juice, sour cream, sugar, flour, vanilla, salt, egg, and cinnamon. Mix well and place in a crust lined baking dish. Top with pie crust or a streusel topping. Bake at 375° for 1 hour or until crust is light brown and apples are soft.

Streusel Topping:
Combine 1/3 cup unbleached flour, 1/3 cup unbleached sugar, and 3 tablespoons softened butter. Rub together until crumbly. Sprinkle on top of pie and bake.

Suggestion: If you have trouble rolling out pie dough on a floured board, try using oil on the board or wax paper or plastic wrap.

Suggestion: When making a pie crust, make a double batch. Roll out crusts and place in a pie dish and freeze. If you have more than one crust place wax paper between them.

Suggestion: If freezing leftover dough in a ball, thaw a day before using. If dough is still too stiff, microwave for 20 seconds. It will soften and make it easier to roll out.

Hint: Add 7 drops of lemon juice or apple cider vinegar to whipping cream to make sour cream.

Blueberry Pie with Pineapple

2 cups blueberries
1 cup unbleached sugar
1/2 cup crushed pineapple
1/4 cup oatmeal
1/2 cup unbleached flour
1/3 stick butter

Line a pie plate with a puff pastry crust. Combine all ingredients and pour into the unbaked shell. Dab with butter. Top with a second pie crust. Brush top crust with milk and sprinkle with unbleached sugar. Place on a pie drip pan. Bake at 375° for 1 1/2 hours.

Puff Pastry:
Combine 4 cups unbleached flour, 1 teaspoon baking powder, 1 teaspoon sea salt, 1 cup lard, 1 egg, 1 tablespoon vinegar and 5 tablespoons cold filtered water.

Suggestion: To prevent fruit fillings from soaking through the crust, brush bottom crust with egg white before adding the fruit. You may do this to regular pie crusts also.

Hint: Pies bake more evenly if placed in the center of the oven.
To make serving easier butter pie plate before placing crust in the plate.
To make a flakier crust use cream or sour cream in place of water.

Hint: Lard or butter will make a flakier pastry or pie crust. Use lard to replace butter. However, do not use oleo to replace butter or lard in a recipe. It may make it tough.

Hint: Mix cinnamon, sugar, and nutmeg with cream and use on fruit or fruit pie.

Cottage Pie

Crust:
1/2 cup cottage cheese
1 egg
2 teaspoons lemon juice
1 cup canola oil
2 Tablespoons unbleached sugar for top
1 teaspoon pure vanilla
1/2 teaspoon sea salt
2 cups unbleached flour
2 tablespoons butter

For the crust, use a blender to process cottage cheese, egg, lemon juice, oil, sugar, vanilla, and salt. Add flour and butter. Mix until well blended and chill in refrigerator for 1 hour. Grease a pie plate. Roll dough to fit plate. Press dough gently in the plate. Fill with cherry filling. Bake at 375° for 1 hour. If crust is not tan increase temperature to 400° for a few minutes longer.

Filling:
5 cups pitted, sour cherries
1 cup unbleached sugar
3 tablespoons cornstarch
2 tablespoons lemon juice
1/4 teaspoon pure almond extract
1 tablespoons milk

Mix cherries, sugar, cornstarch, lemon juice, and almond extract. Spoon into crust. Cover with pie dough cut into strips and woven into lattice design. Brush with milk and sprinkle with unbleached sugar.

Fruit Medley Pie

4 fresh peaches, peeled and sliced
2 nectarines, peeled and sliced
1 cup seedless grapes, cut in half
1 cup fresh pineapple, chunked
1 cup unbleached sugar
1/2 cup rolled oats
1/2 cup unbleached flour
1/3 stick butter

Place all ingredients in a bowl and mix well. Spoon into a pastry lined pie plate. Dab with butter. Cover with crust. Brush with milk and sprinkle with unbleached sugar. Bake at 350° for 2 hours or until done.

Suggestion: Add 1 teaspoon tapioca to fruit pies to prevent spill over.

Suggestion: Add 1/4 teaspoon pure almond extract.

Nectarine Cherry Pie

6 nectarines
1 cup pitted black cherries
4 slices pineapple, cut up
1 cup unbleached sugar
1/2 cup unbleached flour
1/2 cup rolled oats
1 teaspoon lime or lemon juice
1/3 stick butter

Peel and slice nectarines. Place in bowl and add cherries, pineapple, sugar, flour, oats and lime juice. Mix well. Pour into a crust lined pie plate; dab with butter and cover with a top crust. Brush crust with milk and sprinkle with sugar. Bake at 375° for 1 1/2 hours.

Butter Pie Crust:
Combine 2 1/2 cups unbleached flour, 1 teaspoon sea salt, 1 teaspoon unbleached sugar, 1 cup butter, and 1/2 cup filtered water or cream. Chill for 1 hour and then roll out. Place crust in a glass pie plate and bake at 350° for 20 minutes or until lightly tanned.

Peach Pie

1 cup unbleached sugar
1/2 cup unbleached flour
1/8 teaspoon cinnamon
6 fresh peaches, peeled and sliced
2 tablespoons butter

Mix all ingredients except butter. Pour peach mixture into the pastry lined pie plate and dab with butter. Top with crust. Make slits in top crust. Brush top crust with milk and sprinkle with unbleached sugar. Bake at 375° for 1 1/2 hours or until done.

My Favorite Pie Crust:
Mix together 3 cups unbleached flour, 1 cup lard, 1 egg, 1 tablespoon apple cider vinegar, 1 teaspoon sea salt and 5 tablespoons cold filtered water. Dough should be refrigerated overnight.

Suggestion: Add 1/4 teaspoon almond extract to peach or cherry pie.

Variation: Use pears in place of peaches.

Variation: Add 1/2 cup raisins or dried cherries to fruit pies.

Strawberry Pie

1 quart fresh berries
1 cup filtered water
3 tablespoons pure cornstarch
1 tablespoon lemon juice
1/4 teaspoon sea salt
1 cup unbleached sugar

Crush half of the berries and mix with water and cornstarch. Add lemon juice, salt, and sugar. Cook until thick, stirring constantly. Cool. Place remaining berries into a baked pie shell. Pour cooked mixture over berries. Top with whipped cream and serve.

Hint: A pinch of salt will help firm cream when whipped.

Suggestion: When a recipe calls for sour cream or whipped cream use 100% pure dairy products.

Suggestion: Add 1 tablespoon gelatin dissolved in 1 tablespoons hot filtered water to 2 cups cream and whip. Refrigerate 3 to 4 hours.

Suggestion: Add a small amount of honey to whipped cream.

Basic Vanilla Pie Filling

3/4 cup unbleached sugar
1/3 cup unbleached flour
1/8 teaspoon sea salt
2 tablespoons butter
2 eggs
2 cups milk, scalded
1 teaspoon pure vanilla

Combine sugar, flour, salt, butter, and eggs. Slowly add scalded milk. Stir and cook until thick. Add vanilla. If you prefer, use a double boiler. Pour into a baked pastry shell. Top with meringue.

Cooked Meringue
1 tablespoon pure cornstarch
2 tablespoons filtered water
1/2 cup boiling filtered water
3 egg whites
6 tablespoons fructose
1/8 teaspoon sea salt
1 teaspoon pure vanilla

Dissolve cornstarch in cold water. Add boiling water and cook until clear and thick. Let cool completely. Beat egg whites until frothy. Gradually beat in fructose. Beat until stiff. Turn to low and beat in salt and vanilla. Beat in cold cornstarch mixture on high for 1 minute. Spread meringue on pie. Bake at 350° for 10 minutes or until tanned.

Cream Pie

Banana
Slice 2 to 3 ripe bananas and place them in the baked pie shell. Pour basic vanilla cream pie filling over bananas. Top with whipped cream and slices of banana.

Carob or Chocolate
Use basic vanilla pie recipe and add 1/4 cup carob or chocolate powder. Top with meringue or whipped cream.

Coconut
Add 1 cup shredded coconut to basic vanilla cream pie recipe and top with whipped cream or meringue. Sprinkle with 1/4 cup coconut.

Pineapple
Stir 1 cup crushed, drained pineapple (use pineapple that is canned in its own juice or sweetened with honey) into basic vanilla cream pie recipe. Pour into a baked pie shell and top with whipped cream.

Raisin
Add 1 cup soft fresh raisins to basic vanilla cream pie recipe. Raisins can be softened by cooking them in a little filtered water. Drain well.

Hint: Rinse saucepan with water before cooking pudding; this will help to keep it from sticking.

Hint: Sprinkle pie crust with a little unbleached sugar before adding pie filling. This will keep the crust from getting soggy.

Custard Pie

4 eggs
2/3 cup unbleached sugar
1/2 teaspoon sea salt
1/4 teaspoon nutmeg
1 teaspoon pure vanilla
3 cups scalded milk

Blend eggs well. Add sugar, salt, nutmeg, and vanilla. Slowly add milk, stirring continuously. Pour into a pastry lined pie plate. Bake at 400° until a knife inserted into the pie comes out clean. Cool and serve.

Buttery Pie Crust:
Combine 2 1/2 cups unbleached flour, 1 teaspoon sea salt, 1 teaspoon unbleached sugar, 1 cup butter, and 1/2 cup filtered water. Mix well and chill in refrigerator overnight.

Suggestion: Dip knife in warm water before cutting cream or custard pies.

Hint: If you are out of cream try adding 1 tablespoon lemon juice to 3/4 cup milk and whip. Place in freezer for a while before whipping but do not freeze. You may use evaporated milk. Chill and whip but do not use lemon juice.

Lemon Meringue Pie

1 cup fructose
1/4 cup pure cornstarch
1 1/2 cups cold filtered water
3 egg yolks
1 lemon rind, grated
1/4 cup lemon juice
1/8 teaspoon sea salt

Combine fructose and cornstarch. Add water, lemon juice, and salt. Cook and stir. Beat egg yolks and stir in half of the cooked mixture. Stir well and return to pan with remaining hot mixture. Mix and pour into a baked pie shell. Top with meringue and bake at 350° for 15 minutes or until meringue is lightly tanned.

Meringue:
Beat 3 egg whites and 1/4 teaspoon cream of tartar until stiff peaks form. Gradually add 1/3 cup fructose and beat until whites hold stiff peaks. Pour on top of pie and bake at 325° until meringue is tanned.

Suggestion: In place of cream of tartar use a pinch of sea salt

Hint: To make a high meringue add baking powder to egg white before beating.

Suggestion: Leave meringue pie in oven after you shut oven off to keep meringue from weeping.

Hint: When making meringue, add 1 teaspoon apple cider vinegar to the egg whites before beating.

Suggestion: Cut cream pies with a buttered knife.

Suggestion: It is best to use glass or ceramic pie plates.

Pecan Pie

1 1/2 cups brown sugar, packed
2 1/2 tablespoons flour
1/4 cup butter
5 eggs
1/4 cup molasses
1 1/3 cup corn syrup
1 1/2 teaspoons vanilla
1/4 cup molasses
2 1/2 cups pecans

Beat sugar, flour, butter, and eggs. Stir in molasses, syrup, and vanilla. Mix until smooth. Place pecans in an unbaked whole wheat pie crust lined pie plate. Pour egg mixture on top. The nuts will rise to the top during baking. Bake at 350° for 1 hour or until set.

Whole Wheat Pie Crust:
1 cup whole wheat flour
1 tablespoons unbleached sugar
1/2 teaspoon sea salt
1/3 cup canola oil
2 tablespoons cold water

Combine flour, sugar, and salt. Add oil and water. Form dough into a ball. Use for single crust. Roll out and line a pie plate, flute the edges and prick in several places. Bake at 400° for 25 minutes. Use for precooked or cream pies.

Pumpkin Pie

1 1/2 cups prepared squash or pumpkin
1 cup half and half
1 cup unbleached sugar
1/4 teaspoon sea salt
1/4 teaspoon nutmeg
1/4 teaspoon all spice
1/4 teaspoon ginger
1/2 teaspoon cinnamon
2 eggs
1 tablespoons butter, melted

Mix all ingredients and pour into a pastry lined pie dish. Bake at 400° for 1 hour or until a knife inserted comes out clean. Cool and serve with whipped cream.

Variation:
Mix 1 1/4 cups chopped walnuts, and 3/4 cup brown sugar. Sprinkle three-fourths of the mixture into the pastry lined pie plate before adding the pumpkin mixture. When pie is baked, add 3 tablespoons butter to the remaining nut mixture and sprinkle on top of cooled pie.

Suggestion: Adding a little sugar to a cup of black walnuts when grinding or chopping them will keep them from sticking to the grinder or chopper.

Suggestion: Place beaters and bowl in the refrigerator 30 minutes before beating cream. A pinch of salt will help cream whip.

Comments: Lard makes pie crusts flakier. You can render your own lard if you have a pig butchered. You may ask the butcher at the meat locker (slaughter house) to render it for you or buy it from them. Also ask for the cracklings from the lard. They are good in many recipes.

Desserts

Apple Desserts/Cobbler/Pudding/Sauces

Baked Apples

Apple Dumplings

Peach Cobbler

Old Fashioned Bread Pudding

Rice Pudding

Tapioca Pudding

Thickened Apricot Sauce

Blueberry Sauce

Creamy Caramel Sauce

Cream Sauce

Marshmallow Sauce

Baked Apples

6 apples
6 tablespoons unbleached sugar
Nutmeg
1 tablespoons butter
Filtered water

Wash and core apples. Place in a baking dish. Fill hole in apple with 1 tablespoon sugar. Sprinkle apples with nutmeg. Place a pat of butter in each apple. Pour 1/2 cup water around apples. Bake at 325° for 3 hours. Serve with cream.

Apple Dumplings

4 ripe baking apples
1 pie crust dough recipe
4 Tablespoons unbleached sugar
4 pats butter
Cinnamon
4 pats of butter for top of apple dumpling
1/4 cup filtered water for the pan
1/2 cup pure maple syrup to drizzle

Core, wash, and peel apples. Roll out pastry dough. Cut squares large enough to wrap around each apple. Before wrapping place sugar, butter, and cinnamon into the center in the apple. Wrap each apple and place in a baking dish. Place a pat of butter on top of wrapped apple. Sprinkle with 1/2 cup filtered water and drizzle with 1/4 cup pure maple syrup. Bake 425° for 45 minutes.

Peach Cobbler

1 cup unbleached flour
1 teaspoon baking powder
1/8 teaspoon sea salt
1 tablespoons butter
1/4 cup milk
6 peach halves, peeled
1/3 cup unbleached sugar
1/4 teaspoon pure vanilla

Combine flour, baking powder, and salt. Cut in butter. Add milk. Place on floured board and knead lightly. Pat dough to 1-inch thick. Place peaches in a baking dish. Sprinkle with sugar. Place dough on top of peaches. Cut a slit in crust to allow steam to escape. Bake at 450° for 30 minutes. Boil 1/4 cup water and 1/4 cup unbleached sugar for 4 minutes. Stir in 1/4 teaspoon pure vanilla. Pour over cobbler after it has baked for 20 minutes. Bake for an additional 10 minutes. Serve with cream.

Hint: To peel peaches, dip peaches in boiling water for 1 minute. Immediately place peaches into cold water to stop them from cooking. Peel will slip off easy.

Variation: Use apples in place of peaches.

Old Fashioned Bread Pudding

2 cups homemade bread cubes, dried
2 cups milk or half and half
1/4 cup unbleached sugar
3 tablespoons butter
Dash sea salt
2 eggs
1/2 teaspoon pure vanilla

Place bread cubes in a baking dish. Heat milk, sugar, butter, and salt. Beat eggs and add to milk mixture. Stir in vanilla. Pour over bread cubes in baking dish. Place baking dish in shallow pan of water and bake for 45 minutes at 350°. Serve with lemon sauce.

Lemon Sauce:
Combine 1/2 cup fructose, 1 tablespoons pure cornstarch, and a dash of sea salt. Stir in 1 cup filtered water and 1 1/2 teaspoons grated lemon rind. Cook over medium heat for 2 minutes. Stir continuously. Remove from heat and stir in 1 tablespoon butter. Spoon over bread pudding.

Orange Sauce:
Follow directions for lemon sauce but use the juice and rind from 1 orange. Also use only 1/2 cup water.

Rice Pudding

1 quart milk
1/2 cup rice
3 egg yolks
Dash sea salt
1/2 cup unbleached sugar
1 teaspoon pure vanilla
Egg whites
1 tablespoons fructose
1/2 cup seedless raisins

Place milk and rice in a double boiler. Cook for 1 hour or until rice is tender. Beat egg yolks. Mix yolks with a small amount of the rice mixture. Stir and pour back into pot of rice. Add salt, sugar, and vanilla. Place in baking dish. Beat together egg whites and fructose. Pour on top of rice and bake until egg whites are light brown.

Tapioca Pudding

2 egg yolks
2 cups milk
2 tablespoons unbleached sugar
2 tablespoons Tapioca
1/4 teaspoon sea salt
1 teaspoon pure vanilla
2 egg whites
1/2 teaspoon cream of tartar
1/4 cup fructose

Combine yolks, milk, sugar, tapioca, and salt. Stirring constantly cook over medium low heat. Cool and stir in vanilla. Beat egg whites and cream of tartar until frothy. Add fructose to egg mixture. Beat until soft peaks form. Fold into pudding.

Thickened Apricot Sauce

1 tablespoon unbleached flour
1/3 cup unbleached sugar
1 cup apricot juice
1 cup chopped apricots
1 tablespoon butter

Combine flour and sugar. Add juice. Cook over hot water or in a double boiler. Add apricots and butter. Use on bread pudding, ham, rice. This sauce can also be spread on bread.

Blueberry Sauce

1/2 cup unbleached sugar
1/4 cup orange juice
2 tablespoons cornstarch
3 cups blueberries
1 tablespoons ginger

Combine sugar, juice, and cornstarch. Cook and stir until smooth. Add blueberries and ginger. Cook for 2 minutes. Use on waffles, pancakes, pound cake, or ice cream.

Creamy Caramel Sauce

½ cup filtered water
2 cups raw sugar or unbleached
1 ½ cups whipping cream
2 tablespoons butter
1 teaspoon lemon juice

Combine water and sugar in a saucepan. Cook over medium heat until sugar water reaches a boil. Don't stir. Scrape sugar from sides to eliminate crystals. Cook until amber colored. Reduce to low heat. Gradually add cream, stirring with a wooden spoon. Add butter and lemon juice. Cool and use over bread pudding. Sauce can be stored in refrigerator one week.

Cream Sauce

1 cup cream
1 egg white
3 egg yolks
1 cup unbleached sugar
1 teaspoon pure vanilla

Mix first four ingredients. Cook in double boiler until smooth. Stir in vanilla. Serve over bread pudding, gingerbread, or coffee cake.

Variation: Add ¼ cup lemon juice and ⅓ cup coconut.

Variation: Add 3 tablespoons lemon juice and 1 teaspoon grated lemon rind.

Marshmallow Sauce

1/2 cup fructose
3/4 cup light corn syrup
1/4 cup filtered water
2 egg whites at room temperature

Combine fructose, corn syrup, and water. Cook to 238° (soft-ball) stage, approximately 7 minutes. Remove from heat. Whip egg whites until peaks form. With mixer running, pour hot syrup around the inner edge of the bowl, slowly and evenly. Beat until thoroughly mixed. Sauce will be shiny and fluffy. Use on homemade ice cream.

Sandwiches

Camp Sandwich or Backyard Picnic

Chicken Salad Sandwich

Chicken and Tongue Sandwich

Cream Cheese Peanut Butter and Jelly Sandwich,

Lettuce Peanut Butter Honey Mayo Sandwich (LPBHMS)

Peanut Butter and Pickle Sandwich

Egg Salad Sandwich

Grilled Cheese

Grilled Ham Salad Sandwich

Hot Beef, Chicken, or Pork Sandwich,

Sloppy Beef Sandwich

Salmon Sandwich

Terriyaki Hamburg

Camp Sandwich or Barbeque Picnic

Take a large round loaf of homemade rye bread and slice in half widthwise. Hollow out the center, top and bottom. Spread butter on inside of top half, spread mayonnaise on inside of bottom half. Place lettuce leaves in bottom half, top with slices of roast beef. Spread horseradish sauce on the beef. Add slices of Swiss cheese or any natural cheese. Spread with honey mustard. Add slices of chicken breast and spread with mayonnaise. Add layer of provolone cheese slices. Spread softened cream cheese (add cream if needed to make spreadable) and add tomato slices. If desired, pickle can also be added. Place top half on sandwich. Cut into pie wedges and serve. This is a perfect sandwich for camping.

Hint: Spreading butter on the bread first will keep sandwich from getting soggy.

Chicken Salad Sandwich

2 cups cooked chicken, cooled and chopped
Pinch sea salt
2 pickles, chopped
1 rib celery, chopped
1/2 cup mayonnaise
2 tablespoons sour cream

Mix all ingredients and serve with your favorite homemade bread. Add a little chicken broth to moisten salad if needed.

Chicken and Tongue Sandwich

Cook beef tongue until tender. Peel outer layer off, slice, and arrange on slices of bread that has been spread with mayonnaise and honey mustard. Add slices of cooked chicken and a slice of natural cheese. Close sandwich and cut in quarters. Secure with round toothpicks and serve with pickles and home fried potato chips.

Cream Cheese Peanut Butter and Jelly Sandwich

1/4 cup unbleached sugar
6 ounces cream cheese
Peanut butter (natural)
Jam or jelly (homemade or all natural)

Cream together sugar and cream cheese. Spread on slice of fresh homemade bread. Spread second slice of bread with creamy or chunky peanut butter. Spread with jam or jelly and close sandwich. Cut and serve.

Hint: If you make your own peanut butter you can add peanut oil and honey or unbleached sugar.

LPBHMS

Lettuce **P**eanut **B**utter **H**oney **M**ayo **S**andwich

Spread mayo on a slice of fresh homemade bread. Top with a piece of lettuce. Spread another slice of bread with peanut butter and top with honey. Close the sandwich. Cut in half and serve.

Peanut Butter and Pickle Sandwich

Spread fresh slice of homemade bread with peanut butter. Add slices of dill pickle and close sandwich. Serve.

Variation: Spread one slice of bread with peanut butter and add a whole dill pickle. Eat sandwich like a hot dog.

Egg Salad Sandwich

2 eggs
2 tablespoons mayonnaise
Pinch sea salt
Dash pepper
1 tablespoons finely chopped celery
1 teaspoon finely chopped sweet onion

Boil eggs. Cool. Peel and mash. Add mayonnaise, salt, pepper, celery, and onion. Add more mayonnaise if needed. Serve on fresh baked bread.

Grilled Cheese

Spread one side of a slice of bread with butter. Add your favorite slices of natural cheese to unbuttered side. Top with a slice of bread that has been spread with butter. Fry buttered sides on medium heat until light brown.

Variation: Mix equal parts of mayonnaise and cream cheese and add to inside of sandwich.

Grilled Ham Salad Sandwich

Grind home smoked ham. Mix with pickle relish, mayonnaise, and minced onion. Make sandwich with 2 slices of homemade bread that has been spread with butter on the outside. Grill in a frying pan until lightly browned.

Hot Beef, Chicken or Pork Sandwich

Roast meat (slowly) until very done. Use drippings to make gravy. Lay a slice of homemade bread on a plate. Top with thin slices of meat and pour gravy on top. Serve with mashed potatoes.

Sloppy Beef Sandwich

2 pounds ground chuck
1 sweet onion, chopped
1 cup catsup
1 small can tomato paste
1 teaspoon mustard
1 teaspoon apple cider vinegar
1 teaspoon Worcestershire sauce
½ cup filtered water
1 tablespoon unbleached sugar

Brown meat and onion. Add remaining ingredients. Simmer and serve on homemade bread. You can also make hamburger buns from the bread dough if you prefer.

Salmon Sandwich

8 ounces cooked salmon, 1 tablespoons minced sweet onion, 1 tablespoons minced celery and 1/2 cup mayonnaise or more to moisten. Mix well and serve on fresh homemade bread.

Variation: Use smoked salmon and prepare the same way. Use in a sandwich or on crackers.

Terriyaki Hamburg

1/8 cup soy sauce
1/3 cup mayo
1/4 cup honey
1/8 cup Worcestershire sauce
2 garlic cloves, pressed
1/2 teaspoon sea salt
1/4 teaspoon pepper
2 pounds ground chuck
Sweet onion slices

Mix 2 teaspoons soy sauce with mayonnaise. Set aside. Combine honey and remaining soy sauce with Worcestershire sauce, garlic, salt, and pepper. Stir into beef and shape into patties. Fry on grill. Serve on homemade buns with mayonaise mixture and slices of sweet onion.

Soups

Asparagus Soup (Creamy)

1 cup chopped asparagus
1 cup filtered water
2 cups thin white sauce
1/2 teaspoon sea salt
1/4 teaspoon white pepper
1/2 cup cream
1 tablespoons butter
Pinch cayenne

Cook asparagus in water. Add white sauce, salt, and pepper. Bring to boil and add cream and butter. Serve with a pinch of cayenne.

Variation: Instead of white sauce, use 3 cups chicken broth thickened with 2 tablespoons unbleached flour.

Variation: Use 2 tablespoons ground cracklings or fried side pork. Fry and drain. Fry a small chopped onion in the side pork then add to the soup.

White Sauce recipe is located in the cheese sauce section of this book.

Bean Soup with Black Beans

1 1/2 cups black beans
1 sweet onion, chopped
1/4 cup cracklings or butter
2 ribs celery, chopped
1 bay leaf
1/2 teaspoon thyme
1 tablespoon snipped parsley
1 teaspoon sea salt
1/8 teaspoon pepper
8 cups beef broth
1 tablespoons apple cider vinegar

Soak beans 3 hours. Drain and rinse. Sauté onion in butter or cracklings for 2 minutes. Add celery and sauté for 3 minutes. Add beans, bay leaf, thyme, parsley, salt and pepper. Simmer for 2 minutes. Remove bay leaf. Pour mixture into the pot of beef broth. Cover and simmer for 2 hours. Puree 1/2 of the mixture in a blender and return to pot with remaining soup. Heat and add vinegar. Serve.

Suggestion: Serve with shredded cheddar cheese and fresh chopped onion.

Beef Vegetable Soup

1 pound beef, cubed
1 tablespoons olive oil
2 cups tomatoes, diced
3 cups filtered water
2 potatoes, peeled and diced
1 onion, diced
2 ribs celery, diced
1/2 cup leaves from celery, chopped
1/4 cup fresh snipped parsley
2 carrots, sliced
1 teaspoon sea salt
1/4 teaspoon fresh ground pepper

Brown meat in olive oil. Place in a large kettle with remaining ingredients and bring to a boil. Lower heat and simmer for 4 hours.

Variation: Add 1/2 cup barley.

Variation: This can be made with ground beef.

Variation: Add 4 cups milk and 1/3 cup flour just before serving.

Cabbage Soup

5 cups shredded white cabbage
1 sweet onion, chopped
2 tablespoons butter
3 tablespoons cracklings or fried side pork (ground or cubed)
3 carrots, sliced
2 potatoes, peeled and diced
2 ribs celery, chopped
2 cups tomatoes, diced
1 teaspoon sea salt
1/4 teaspoon white pepper
1 tablespoon snipped parsley

Fry onions in butter. Place onions and cabbage in a large cooking pot with remaining ingredients. Cook for 1 hour.

Variation: Soup may be thickened with white sauce. Add 1/2 cup of rolled oats will also thicken the soup.

Cheese Soup with Broccoli

½ cup minced onion
1 tablespoon butter
5 cups chicken broth
1 pound chopped broccoli
1 clove garlic, pressed
4 cups milk
½ pound natural jack cheese, shredded
½ pound natural sharp cheddar cheese, shredded

Sauté onion in butter. Add broth and boil. Stir in broccoli and garlic. Cook for 4 minutes. Add milk and cheese. Simmer until cheeses melt. Serve.

Variation: For a richer soup add 2 egg yolks. Beat yolks and add a little of the hot soup; when mixture is well blended stir into remaining soup.

Variation: For carrot soup add 1 cup cooked, diced carrots

Variation: For cauliflower soup add a small head of chopped, cooked cauliflower.

Chicken Soup

1 large chicken or 3 pounds of chicken pieces
2 carrots, sliced thick
1 onion, diced
2 ribs celery
2 tablespoons snipped parsley
2 teaspoons sea salt
1/4 teaspoon pepper
Pinch of saffron stamens or 1/2 teaspoon saffron powder
2 quarts filtered water

Place chicken in a kettle with the rest of the ingredients. Add water and bring to a boil. Reduce heat to medium and simmer for 2 hours. Skim foam from top. Remove chicken. It is easiest to remove fat from soup by cooling soup in refrigerator. Fat will come to the top and can be easily removed. Fat can be saved for other uses. Add noodles to soup and cook until noodles are soft.

Suggestion: If you are using homemade noodles you may want to cook them in filtered water until tender. Drain and rinse noodles before adding to the soup. Homemade noodles tend to thicken the soup.

Suggestion: Adding a teaspoon of apple cider vinegar enhances the flavor. This enables you to reduce the amount of salt.

Suggestion: You can use rice in the place of noodles. Basmati or brown rice are the most nutritious. To make rice tender let it stand in water for 1 hour before cooking. Cook rice in filtered water. Add to the soup.

Hint: A leaf of lettuce will help remove fat from the top of soup. Remove as much grease as you can then add the lettuce for a few minutes.

Comment: Saffron stamens from Spain are very expensive but are very good in soup. Powdered Mexican saffron is much cheaper. You can use 1/2 to 1 teaspoon in a kettle of soup.

Chili

1 cup pinto or kidney beans
Filtered water
1 teaspoon baking soda
2 pounds ground chuck or Hamburg
1 onion, chopped
2 cloves garlic, pressed
1 1/2 teaspoons sea salt
3 cups diced tomatoes
1 pepper, chopped
1 teaspoon cumin
2 tablespoons chili powder

Cook beans according to directions on package. Add a teaspoon of baking soda to the first water rinse; cover with water and cook. Brown meat, add onion, garlic, and salt. Cook 5 minutes then add to cooked beans. Add tomatoes, chopped pepper, cumin, and chili powder. Cook for 1 hour.

Hint: If you add too much garlic to the soup or chili, tie a bunch of parsley together. Add parsley to the soup and cook it awhile.

Hint: If soup or chili is too salty add a little brown sugar, a whole peeled apple, potato or tomato. Place in soup or chili and let it cook awhile. Remove.

Hint: If you are out of chili powder you can make your own. Mix cumin, oregano, chili pepper, sea salt, cayenne pepper, garlic powder, and allspice. Mix a teaspoon of each. Use to taste.

Clam Chowder New England Style

1/4 pound salt pork, diced
1 onion, chopped
6 potatoes, peeled and chopped
1/2 teaspoon sea salt
Fresh ground pepper
2 tablespoons butter
1 pint clams, chopped
1 tablespoons unbleached flour
3 cups milk
1 cup cream
2 cups thin white sauce
1/2 teaspoon Worcestershire sauce (optional)

Brown salt pork in frying pan. Discard most of the fat. Add onions, potatoes, salt, and pepper to the pork. Stir and cook until vegetables are tender. Melt butter in a small frying pan. Add clams and fry. Add flour and stir. Add clam mixture to vegetables. Stir in milk, cream, and white sauce. Add Worcestershire sauce and stir.

Creamy Mushroom Soup

1 cup mushrooms, chopped
1 tablespoons minced onion
2 tablespoons butter
2 cups thin white sauce
1 cup chicken broth
1/2 teaspoon sea salt
1/4 teaspoon pepper
Paprika

Cook mushrooms and onions in butter. Add white sauce, chicken broth, salt, and pepper. Cook over hot water (double boiler) for 10 minutes and serve. Garnish with paprika.

Onion Soup, French Style

1 pound sliced onions
2 tablespoons butter
1 teaspoon sea salt
1/4 teaspoon pepper
3 cups beef broth
3 cups chicken broth
Croutons, homemade
6 slices all natural provolone cheese

Sauté onions in butter. Add salt and pepper. Add broth. Simmer and serve with croutons and cheese slices.

Croutons are in the appetizer section in this book.

Oyster Stew

1/2 cup butter
1/4 cup chopped sweet onion
3 cups fresh oysters, shucked
1 teaspoon sea salt
1/8 teaspoon pepper
1/8 teaspoon Worcestershire sauce
2 cups milk
1 cup half and half
1/2 cup cream
1 tablespoon snipped parsley

Melt butter and fry onions and oysters. Add salt, pepper, and Worcestershire sauce. Cook for 10 minutes. Oysters will curl on the edges. Keep oysters hot while heating milk, half and half, and cream. Do not boil. Add oysters to hot milk and serve. Sprinkle with parsley.

Pork Hock Bean Soup

2 pounds navy beans
Filtered water
1 teaspoon baking soda
4 quarts filtered water
4 pork hocks or bone from a home smoked ham
1 onion, chopped
2 ribs celery, diced
1 teaspoon ginger
1 teaspoon sea salt
1/4 teaspoon pepper
1 teaspoon apple cider vinegar

Cover beans with filtered water, bring to boil and add a teaspoon baking soda. Stir mixture when it froths. Remove from heat. Let sit for 1 hour. Drain. Add 4 quarts filtered water, hocks, onion, celery, ginger, salt, pepper, and vinegar. Bring to a boil and simmer for 3 hours or until hocks are tender.

Potato Soup

2 cups chicken broth
1 teaspoon sea salt
4 potatoes, diced
1 sweet onion, chopped
2 tablespoons butter
1/4 teaspoon pepper
1/4 cup unbleached flour
1 cup milk
1 cup cream

Cook broth and salt to taste. Add potatoes, onion, butter, and pepper. Dissolve flour in a little of the milk. Add to milk and cream. Stir milk mixture into the soup and simmer. Do not boil.

Sauces/Dressing/Marinade Sauces

Cheese Sauce

1 cup milk
2 tablespoons butter
2 tablespoons unbleached flour
1 cup milk
2 shakes paprika
1/8 teaspoon pepper
3/4 teaspoon sea salt
1 egg yolk
2 tablespoons grated natural cheddar cheese

Melt butter and stir in flour. Gradually add milk. Shake in paprika, pepper, and salt. Cook and stir. Mix egg yolk with a little of the hot mixture. Pour egg yolk mixture back into the pan and cook until thick. Use on macaroni, fish, rice, or veggies.

Cheesy Tomato Sauce

2 tablespoons unbleached flour
1 cup tomato juice
1 tablespoons lemon juice
1/2 cup grated cheese
1/2 teaspoon sea salt
1/2 cup homemade buttered bread crumbs

Mix flour and a small amount of tomato juice until it forms a paste. Add remaining tomato juice and lemon juice. Cook and simmer. Add grated cheese and salt. Stir and serve over cooked veggies. Top with buttered bread crumbs.

Creamy Dillweed Sauce

2 teaspoons cornstarch
2 tablespoons filtered water
1/2 cup sour cream
1 teaspoon fresh dill weed
1/4 teaspoon sea salt
Dash pepper

Dissolve cornstarch in water. Combine cream, dill weed, salt, and pepper. Add cornstarch mixture. Cook on medium for 5 minutes or until thick. Use on fish, salmon patties, and vegetables.

Curry Cream Sauce

1 cup sour cream
1/4 cup mayonnaise
1 tablespoon grated onion
1 tablespoon mustard
1 teaspoon Worcestershire sauce
1/2 teaspoon curry powder
1/2 teaspoon sea salt
1/2 teaspoon pepper
Hot sauce (optional)

Mix all ingredients. Serve with tomato. Cut tomato in six sections. Cut tomato only to the core. Place a large scoop of the mixture into the center.

Suggestion: Be creative. Try on different foods like eggs and sandwiches.

White Sauce

Thin White Sauce
Melt 1 tablespoons butter. Stir in 1 tablespoons unbleached flour. Gradually add 1 cup milk. Cook on medium, stirring constantly. You may also cook sauce in a double boiler. Add 1/2 teaspoon sea salt and a dash of pepper. Cook until smooth. Use in cream soups.

Medium White Sauce
Melt 2 tablespoons butter. Stir in 2 tablespoons flour. Add 1 cup milk gradually. Cook on medium stirring constantly or cook in a double boiler. Add 1/2 teaspoon sea salt and a dash of pepper. Cook until smooth. Use for scalloped dishes.

Thick White Sauce
Melt 3 tablespoons butter. Stir in 3 tablespoons unbleached flour. Add 1 cup milk gradually. Cook on medium stirring constantly or cook in a double boiler. Add 1/2 teaspoon sea salt and a dash of pepper. Cook until smooth. Use for soufflés.

Extra Thick White Sauce
Melt 4 tablespoons butter. Stir in 4 tablespoons unbleached flour. Gradually add 1 cup milk. Cook on medium stirring constantly or cook in double boiler. Add 1/2 teaspoon sea salt and a dash of pepper. Cook until smooth. Use for croquettes.

Cheese Spread

1/2 pound natural Cheddar cheese
1/2 pound natural mozzarella cheese
1 small can condensed milk
1/4 cup pimento or red pepper, finely chopped
2 eggs
Pinch sea salt

Mix ingredients and melt in a double boiler. Cool and keep in refrigerator.

Sauces/Dressing/Marinade Sauces

Dressings

Dillweed Dressing

1 cup mayonnaise
1 cup sour cream
1 tablespoon minced onion
1 tablespoon dill weed
1/2 teaspoon seasoned salt
1 teaspoon Worcestershire sauce
2 drops tabasco sauce
1 1/2 tablespoon parsley

Mix all ingredients together. Serve with raw veggies, chips, and over scrambled eggs.

Blue Cheese Dressing

1 (3 ounce) package cream cheese
1/3 cup blue cheese, crumbled
1/4 teaspoon sea salt
1/2 teaspoon garlic powder
1/2 cup mayonnaise
1/2 cup sour cream

Blend ingredients and serve on salad. This can be added to gravy dishes.

Buttermilk Dressing

1/2 cup mayonnaise
1/2 cup buttermilk
1 tablespoon apple cider vinegar
1 tablespoons snipped parsley
1 tablespoons minced sweet onion
1 clove garlic, pressed
1/4 teaspoon sea salt

Place all ingredients in a pint jar and shake until well mixed.

Celery Seed Dressing

2/3 cup unbleached sugar
1/2 cup apple cider vinegar
1/4 cup vegetable oil
1 teaspoon celery seeds

Delicious on any tossed salad, in cole slaw or serve with a mixed raw vegetable dish.

Variation: Poppy Seed Dressing:
Use same ingredients as celery seed dressing except substitute 1 teaspoon of poppy seeds for the celery seeds.

Cole Slaw Dressing

½ cup mayonnaise
4 tablespoons vinegar
3 teaspoons unbleached sugar
1 teaspoon mustard
1 teaspoon sea salt
¼ teaspoon pepper
¼ cup sour cream
1 tablespoons minced onion

Mix well and stir into sliced cabbage.

Dry Salad Dressing Mix

½ cup dried parsley flakes
¼ cup dried chives
1 tablespoon dried dill weed
¼ teaspoon sea salt
⅛ teaspoon pepper

Blend well and refrigerate in a tightly sealed container.

Combine 2 tablespoons mix with ½ cup mayonnaise, ½ cup buttermilk or sour cream. Serve over salad greens or use as a veggie dip.

French Onion Dressing

1 cup olive oil
1/2 cup apple cider vinegar
1 cup catsup (homemade is best)
1 cup unbleached sugar
1 teaspoon paprika
1 teaspoon lemon juice
1 tablespoons minced sweet onion

Blend well. Use on salads or sandwiches.

Honey and Mustard Dressing

1 cup mayonnaise
1/4 cup gourmet mustard or 1 teaspoon dry mustard
1/4 cup honey
2 tablespoons canola oil
3/4 teaspoon apple cider vinegar or 1 tablespoon lemon juice
1/4 teaspoon sea salt
1/4 teaspoon pepper
2 tablespoons minced onion (optional)

Blend well and serve over lettuce. This can also be served with chicken breasts or pork.

Island Dressing

1 cup mayonnaise
1/4 cup unbleached sugar
1/4 cup catsup
1/4 cup sweet pickle relish

Mix well and serve on sandwiches or salads.

Italian Dressing

1/2 cup virgin olive oil
1/3 cup apple cider vinegar
3 cloves garlic cloves, pressed
2 teaspoons Italian seasoning
1 teaspoon unbleached sugar
1/4 teaspoon pepper
1 tablespoon minced onion

Blend well and serve on any combination salad or veggie mixture.

Sauces/Dressing/Marinade Sauces

Marinades/Basting/Serving Sauces

Marinade Basting Sauce

B-B-Q Chicken Marinade Sauce

Marinade Sauce for Steak

B-B-Q Sauce with Garlic

Chili Sauce

Curry Sauce

Lemon Sauce

Mushroom Sauce

Onion Sauce

Raisin Sauce

Sour Cream Mustard Sauce

Marinade Basting Sauce

1 sweet onion, minced
2 tablespoons butter
1 teaspoon sea salt
1 teaspoon pepper
2 tablespoons honey
2 tablespoons brown sugar
1/2 cup cranberry juice
1 tablespoon Worcestershire sauce
1/4 teaspoon dry mustard

Brown onion in butter. Add salt, pepper, honey, sugar, cranberry juice, Worcestershire sauce, and mustard. Simmer for 5 minutes. Marinate or brush on grilled chicken, Cornish hen, or chicken breasts.

B-B-Q Chicken Marinade Sauce

1/2 gallon apple cider vinegar
1/2 pound butter or canola oil
1/2 pound sea salt
1/2 cup Worcestershire sauce
1 tablespoon honey

Cook all ingredients together and keep hot if you wish to use as a spray or in a shaker. Excellent marinade for chicken, pork chops, or steaks. Sauces can be for basting as you grill. Keep only unused portion. Store in refrigerator.

Marinade Sauce for Steak

1 tablespoon fine chopped onion
1/2 teaspoon pepper corns
2 tablespoons apple cider vinegar
2 tablespoons olive oil
2 tablespoons soy sauce or Worcestershire sauce

Mix all ingredients. Pierce steaks with a fork. Place steaks in a tightly sealed bag; add sauce and refrigerate for 2 hours, turning occasionally. Grill.

B-B-Q Sauce with Garlic

2 cloves garlic, pressed
2 teaspoons butter, melted
1 cup catsup (homemade if you have it)
1/4 cup brown sugar
1/4 cup chili sauce
2 tablespoons Worcestershire sauce
1 tablespoon celery seeds
1 tablespoon dry mustard
1/2 teaspoon sea salt
1/4 teaspoon hot sauce

Mix all ingredients together and heat. Brush on ribs or chicken.

Chili Sauce

1 quart tomatoes, peeled and diced
1 rib celery, diced
1 sweet onion, diced
1 small green pepper, diced
1 tablespoons sea salt
1 cup unbleached sugar
1/4 teaspoon pepper
1/3 cup apple cider vinegar
Pinch of cumin
1/4 teaspoon cinnamon
1/4 teaspoon ginger

Place tomatoes, celery, onions, and green pepper in a large kettle and sprinkle with salt. Let sit for 1 hour and simmer over low heat. Stir in remaining ingredients and simmer for 25 minutes. Use on hot dogs and hamburgers or other meats. Remaining sauce can be frozen.

Curry Sauce

3/4 cup sour cream
1/2 cup mayonnaise
1 tablespoon minced onion
1 tablespoon mustard
1 teaspoon Worcestershire sauce
1/2 teaspoon curry powder
1/2 teaspoon sea salt
1/4 teaspoon pepper

Blend ingredients together. Serve with roast beef or chicken.

Lemon Sauce

1 tablespoon butter
1 tablespoon flour
1/4 teaspoon sea salt
1/8 teaspoon white pepper
1/2 cup milk
1/2 teaspoon lemon juice
1/2 teaspoon grated lemon rind

Combine all ingredients and cook for 1 minute. Serve over chicken breast.

Mushroom Sauce

4 tablespoons unbleached flour
4 tablespoons butter
1 1/2 cups chicken or beef broth
1/2 cup filtered water
1/2 teaspoon sea salt
1/4 teaspoon pepper
1 cup sliced mushrooms

Brown flour slightly in melted butter. Add broth, water, salt, and pepper. Cook and stir until thick. Add mushrooms and simmer for 2 minutes. Serve over steak or roast beef.

Onion Sauce

2 tablespoons butter
1 sweet onion, sliced and separated
1 teaspoon mustard
1/4 teaspoon sea salt
1/8 teaspoon white pepper

Melt butter. Add onions and brown slightly. Add remaining ingredients. Simmer for 2 minutes. Use on liver, roast beef, steaks, or meatloaf.

Raisin Sauce

2 cups raisins
1 1/2 cups filtered water
Pinch sea salt
2 cups unbleached sugar
1 tablespoon pure cornstarch
1 tablespoon grated orange rind
3 tablespoons fresh orange juice

Combine raisins, water, and salt. Add sugar, cornstarch, grated rind, and juice. Great on pork and home smoked ham.

Variation: Combine 1 cup raisins, 1 cup homemade jelly, 1 tablespoons grated orange peel and 1 teaspoon mustard. Heat and let stand for 2 hours. Serve on home smoked ham, pork, or roast beef.

Variation: Combine 2 tablespoons butter, 2 tablespoons pure cornstarch, 2 cups orange juice and 1/2 cup raisins. Cook for 1 minute. Serve over meats or with custard pie.

Sour Cream Mustard Sauce

1 1/4 cups sour cream
2 tablespoons mustard
1 teaspoon sea salt
1 teaspoon pepper
3 tablespoons lemon juice

Combine all ingredients. Mix well. Serve on meats, fish, and salad.

Vegetables

Vegetable/Meat/Seafood Salad

Apple Spinach Salad

12 ounces baby spinach
2 apples, chopped
1/2 cup salted cashews
1/4 cup raisins
1/4 cup unbleached sugar
2 tablespoons apple cider vinegar
1/4 cup olive oil
1/4 teaspoon celery salt

Combine spinach, apples, cashews, and raisins. Whisk together sugar, vinegar, oil, and salt. Pour over salad and toss.

Bean Salad

1/2 pound green beans
1/2 pound yellow wax beans
1/2 cup dried black eyed peas
1/2 cup dried navy beans
1/2 cup dried kidney beans
1/2 cup baby lima beans
1 small sweet onion, chopped
1/2 cup apple cider vinegar
1/2 cup olive oil
3 tablespoons thyme
1 large garlic clove, pressed

Cook wax and green beans until tender. Set aside to cool. Cook dried peas and beans, drain and cool. Place cooled beans and peas in a large bowl. Add onion vinegar, oil, thyme, and garlic. Mix well and place in refrigerator overnight.

Broccoli Salad

1 teaspoon unbleached sugar
8 ounces Italian dressing (with no MSG or use homemade)
4 cups broccoli florets
4 carrots, sliced
1 sweet onion, chopped
1 can ripe olives
1 (2 ounce) jar pimento, diced

Dissolve sugar in dressing. Place broccoli, carrots, onion, olives, and pimento in a bowl. Pour dressing on salad and toss.

Carrot Salad

1 cup crushed pineapple
1/2 cup filtered water
1/4 cup unbleached sugar
3 cups shredded carrots
1/2 cup mayonnaise
1/2 cup raisins
1 tablespoons unbleached sugar

Cook pineapple in filtered water and 1/4 cup sugar. Cook for 10 minutes and drain. Reserve juice for other uses. Add carrots, mayonnaise, raisins, and 1 tablespoons sugar. To plump raisins, cook in pineapple juice. Cool, drain, and add to salad. Serve with chicken or turkey.

Creamy Coleslaw

4 cups shredded cabbage
1/4 cup shredded carrots
1/4 cup grated onion
1 teaspoon sea salt
1/4 teaspoon pepper
1/2 teaspoon paprika
1/2 cup mayonnaise
1/2 cup sour cream
1 teaspoon apple cider vinegar
1 tablespoon unbleached sugar
Slivers of green pepper
1 cup crushed pineapple

Mix all ingredients together and let sit for 1 hour before serving.

Great Coleslaw

1 1/2 cup unbleached sugar
1 cup apple cider vinegar
1 cup canola oil
1 tablespoon sea salt
1/2 teaspoon white pepper
1 teaspoon celery seed
3 pounds shredded cabbage
1 sweet onion
1/2 cup shredded carrots
1/2 cup chopped red pepper
1/2 cup chopped green pepper

Combine sugar, vinegar, oil, salt, pepper, and celery seed. Cook until sugar is dissolved. Cool and pour over cabbage, onion, carrots, and peppers. Refrigerate overnight.

Red Skin Potato Salad

4 red skin potatoes
4 new potatoes
1 cup green beans
1 cup yellow beans
1/4 cup sweet onion, chopped
3 tablespoons Olive oil
3 tablespoons apple cider vinegar
1/2 tablespoon dried rosemary
1/4 teaspoon sea salt
1/4 teaspoon pepper
2 tablespoons unbleached sugar

Cook potatoes; cool and dice. Cook beans. Cool beans and cut up. Mix potatoes, beans, and onions together. Combine oil, vinegar, rosemary, salt, pepper, and sugar. Pour over potato mixture; blend well and chill before serving.

Creamy Colibroc Salad

1 1/2 cups broccoli
1 1/2 cups cauliflower
1/2 cup sliced fresh mushrooms
1/2 cup fresh or frozen peas
1 cup mayonnaise
1/2 cup sour cream
1/2 teaspoon sea salt
1/4 teaspoon white pepper
1 garlic clove, pressed
1/2 cup crisp fried bacon, broken (Use bacon from a health food store, vegetable bacon, or home smoked bacon).

Combine all ingredients. Chill 2 hours and serve.

German Potato Salad

3 slices bacon (home smoked)
3 eggs
1/2 cup unbleached sugar
1 tablespoon unbleached flour
1/4 teaspoon sea salt
Dash pepper
1/2 cup filtered water
1/3 cup apple cider vinegar
3 ribs celery, chopped
1 sweet onion, chopped
2 1/2 cups cooked diced potatoes
1/2 cup red sweet pepper diced

Fry bacon until crisp. Drain and crumble. Beat eggs, sugar, flour, salt, and pepper. Stir in water and vinegar. Add to bacon. Cook and stir until thick. Add celery, onions, potatoes, and red pepper. Serve cold or hot.

Layered Salad

Small head of lettuce
1 cup fresh or frozen peas (thawed and drained)
1/2 cup chopped sweet onion
2 ribs celery, chopped
1/4 cup chopped red pepper
1/4 cup chopped green pepper
1 cup mayonnaise
1 cup sour cream
1/4 cup unbleached sugar
2 cups shredded natural Cheddar cheese
1 pound bacon (home smoked) or ground cracklings

Layer the bottom of an oblong glass dish with 1-inch of chopped lettuce. Spread peas evenly across lettuce. Sprinkle with onion, celery, and peppers. Fry bacon until crisp, drain and cool. Break into small pieces and sprinkle on top. Mix mayonnaise, sour cream, and sugar until well blended. Pour evenly over the top of salad and top with the shredded cheese.

Spinach Salad

1 pound spinach
1 head of lettuce
1 cup bean sprouts
½ cup water chestnuts
3 hard boiled eggs
8 thin slices side pork, cut and fried brown (can use home smoked bacon instead)
1 sweet onion, sliced

Clean and cut lettuce and spinach. Add sprouts and chestnuts. Chop eggs and add to salad. Add brown side pork or bacon. Add onion. Toss with dressing.

Dressing:
¾ cup unbleached sugar
¼ cup apple cider vinegar
⅓ cup catsup
½ teaspoon sea salt
2 tablespoons Worcestershire sauce
1 tablespoon minced onion

Mix well and pour over salad.

The Ultimate Salad

1 small head of lettuce, washed and cut
1 bag spinach, washed and cut
1 red sweet pepper
1 yellow sweet pepper
1 orange sweet pepper
1 large carrot, cleaned and sliced
1 cup chopped broccoli
1 cup chopped cauliflower
1 large ripe tomato
1 sweet onion, chopped or sliced
1 cucumber, sliced
1/2 cup crumbled blue cheese

Mix all ingredients together. Top with onion tomato dressing.

Onion Tomato Dressing:
Mix 1 cup catsup (homemade is best), 1/2 cup virgin olive oil, 1 teaspoon sea salt, 2 tablespoons apple cider vinegar, 1/2 cup corn syrup, 1 clove garlic (pressed), 1/2 cup unbleached sugar, 1/2 teaspoon Worcestershire sauce, 1/2 cup finely ground sweet onion, and 1 teaspoon molasses. Stir in blender until sugar is dissolved. Pour over salad and toss.

Hint: You may mix sugar with a little filtered water and cook until dissolved. Add sugar water to remaining mixture. The sugar will dissolve faster.

Vegetable Salad Mold

1/4 cup fructose
1 envelope unflavored gelatin
1/2 teaspoon sea salt
1 1/4 cups filtered water, divided
1/4 cup apple cider vinegar
1 tablespoons lemon juice
1/2 cup finely chopped cabbage
1 cup finely chopped celery
1 tablespoon finely chopped red pepper
1 tablespoon finely chopped green pepper
1 grated shredded carrot

Combine fructose, gelatin, and salt. Add 1/2 cup water; heat on low and stir until dissolved. Remove from heat. Add remaining water, vinegar, and lemon juice. Chill and add cabbage, celery, carrots, and peppers. Place in mold or serving dish. Chill until set solid.

Crab Salad

1/4 cup mayonnaise
1/4 cup sour cream
1 tablespoon chopped pimento
1 tablespoon lemon juice
1/2 teaspoon sea salt
Dash pepper
1 cup diced celery
1 cup diced crab meat

Combine mayonnaise, sour cream, pimento, lemon juice, salt, and pepper. Stir in celery and crab meat. Serve on a bed of lettuce.

There are a variety of lettuces to choose from: butterhead, iceberg, Boston, bib, green leaf, loose leaf, Romaine and red oak leaf.

Glorified Chicken Salad

½ cup sour cream
½ cup mayonnaise
½ cup seedless grapes or raisins
½ cup cashews or walnuts
1 rib celery, sliced
1 apple, cut up
½ cup chunked pineapple, cooked with 1 teaspoon fructose then drained
2 cups cooked chicken, cooled and diced

Blend sour cream and mayonnaise. Add grapes, nuts, celery, apple, and pineapple. Mix well and fold in chicken.

Variation: Turkey can be substituted for chicken.

Molded Salmon Salad

2 tablespoons unflavored gelatin
¼ cup cold filtered water
2 cups boiling filtered water
2 cups shredded red salmon
1¼ cups chopped celery
1 cup finely chopped cabbage
⅔ cup chopped sweet pickle
1½ teaspoons sea salt
1 tablespoon lemon juice
1 tablespoon apple cider vinegar
½ cup mayonnaise

Soften gelatin in cold filtered water. Add hot water. Stir until dissolved. Cool until partially set. Add salmon, celery, cabbage, pickles, salt, lemon juice, vinegar, and mayonnaise. Mix lightly. Press into a mold. Chill until firm. Serve on a bed of lettuce.

Hint: For easier removal, set mold in a pan of hot water for a few minutes.

Taco Salad

1 pound fresh ground chuck
1/4 cup chopped sweet onion
1/4 cup chopped red pepper
1 envelope taco seasoning (with no MSG)
1/4 cup filtered water
1 cup crushed tortilla chips
2 cups refried beans
4 ounces natural Cheddar cheese, shredded

Brown beef, onion, and pepper. Drain. Stir in taco seasoning and water. Cook and stir until thick about 3 to 4 minutes. Set aside. Place chips in a square baking dish. Stir beans until smooth. Spoon evenly over the chips. Bake at 375° for 15 minutes. Top with Cheddar cheese. Other toppings that can be chopped are lettuce, tomato, sliced ripe olives, sour cream and picante sauce.

Vegetables

Asparagus

Heat 1/3 cup butter and 1/3 cup chicken broth (homemade or with no MSG). Add asparagus, 1/2 teaspoon sea salt, and a dash of pepper. Cover and cook 5 minutes.

Variation: Melt 1/2 cup shredded natural Cheddar cheese and 1/2 cup shredded natural white cheese. Add 1/4 cup half and half. Pour over the asparagus. Then top with 2 tablespoons chopped pimento and 2 teaspoons toasted sesame seeds.

Variation: Mix 1/2 cup cream or half and half, stir in 1 tablespoon unbleached flour. Cook over medium heat until thick, stirring constantly. Pour over cooked asparagus.

Baked Beans

1 pound navy beans
1 pound side pork or home smoked bacon
1 rib celery, chopped
1 onion, chopped
1 cup brown sugar
1 cup catsup
1/8 cup molasses
1/2 teaspoon mustard
1/2 teaspoon sea salt
1/8 teaspoon pepper

Cook beans in filtered water according to directions on package. Cut side pork into small cubes and fry; drain and add to the beans. Add celery, onion, brown sugar, catsup, molasses, mustard, salt, and pepper. Mix well. Bake in oven at 325° for 2 hours. Stir occasionally.

Suggestion: When making baked beans you only need to simmer them for 1 hour then bake in a slow oven with the ingredients above.

Variation: Put beans in a pot and cover generously with filtered water. Bring to a boil and add 1 teaspoon baking soda (the water will froth up). Let sit for 1 hour; drain rinse and add enough filtered water to cover beans. Simmer until tender.

Hint: To help tenderize beans add 1 tablespoon apple cider vinegar to the beans when cooking them. Simmer beans so they do not crack.

Beets in Sour Cream

5 medium beets
1 cup filtered water
2 tablespoons butter
2 teaspoons unbleached flour
2 tablespoons apple cider vinegar
1 tablespoon unbleached sugar
1/4 teaspoon sea salt
1/4 teaspoon dill weed
1/8 teaspoon pepper
1/2 cup sour cream
3 tablespoons half and half

Cook beets in water and then slice. Melt butter and blend in flour. Cook over low heat and stir until smooth and bubbly. Remove from heat. Stir in vinegar, sugar, salt, dill weed, and pepper. Return to heat and boil, stirring constantly. Cook for 1 minute. Mix in sour cream and half and half. Simmer over low heat until heated through. Pour over cooked beets.

Hint: If using fresh beets, scrub and cook with tops and roots on to prevent beets from losing their color.

Hot Thickened Beets

6 tablespoons unbleached sugar
3 tablespoons pure cornstarch
1/2 teaspoon sea salt
3 tablespoons butter
1/4 cup filtered water
1/2 cup apple cider vinegar
3 cups sliced or diced beets

Combine sugar, cornstarch, salt, butter, water, and vinegar. Cook until thick and then add beets.

Blossoming Onion

Clean a large sweet onion thoroughly. Cut into sections leaving onion attached at the root. Place in filtered ice water for 2 hours or overnight. Drain. Place the onion into the egg wash (recipe below). Drain. Dust with seasoned flour (recipe below) being careful to get mixture between the petals. Shake off excess. Deep fry onion in hot grease at 350° until light brown. Tear off petals and dip into cayenne dip or horseradish dip.

Egg Wash:
Beat three eggs until frothy and add 1 cup milk; beat. Dip onion blossom.

Seasoned Flour:
Mix 2 cups unbleached flour, 1/4 teaspoon Cajun seasoning and 1/4 teaspoon cayenne pepper, and 1/2 teaspoon sea salt.

Cayenne dip:
Mix 1/2 cup mayonnaise, 1/4 cup sour cream and 1/2 teaspoon cayenne pepper.

Horseradish Dip:
Combine 4 tablespoons mayonnaise, 3 tablespoons horseradish, 2 tablespoons catsup, 1 teaspoon paprika, and a dash hot sauce.

Variation: Use vegetables that have been cleaned and cut into strips. Suggested vegetables are: okra, carrots, celery, zucchini, peppers, and mushrooms.

Carrots and Green Beans

1 pound fresh green beans
1/2 pound baby carrots
1/2 teaspoon sea salt
1/2 teaspoon dill weed
1 cup filtered water
2 tablespoons butter
2 tablespoons diced onion

Cook beans, carrots, salt, and dill weed in filtered water for 10 minutes. Drain. Melt butter over low heat; fry onions until tender. Add vegetables and toss gently.

Variation: Make caramelized veggies. Use green beans, carrots, celery, parsnips, and onions. Toss with 2 tablespoons olive oil and roast for 30 minutes at 500°. Stir occasionally.

Hint: Always wash vegetables in filtered water with salt or apple cider vinegar.

Hint: Dress up green beans by adding butter, basil, lemon pepper, and sea salt.

Hint: Drop carrots in boiling water for 5 minutes and the skin will slide off easily.

Hint: For better flavor, add butter and/or sugar to vegetables when cooking.

Hint: Add a little lemon juice to water when cooking broccoli or cauliflower for a better flavor and color.

Comment: A good way to encourage children to eat their vegetables is to cook the vegetables in chicken broth or to top them with a melted natural cheese.

Marinated Carrots

2 pounds carrots sliced and cooked, crisp tender
1 teaspoon sea salt
1 sweet onion, sliced
1 cup unbleached sugar
1/2 cup apple cider vinegar
1 cup tomato soup (with no MSG available in the supermarket)
1/2 cup canola oil
1/2 teaspoon dry mustard
1/2 cup green pepper, sliced thin
1 teaspoon Worcestershire sauce

Cook carrots in filtered water, with salt, until crisp tender. Slice onions and add to carrots. Mix remaining ingredients and pour over the carrots and onions. Marinate at least 4 hours before serving.

Suggestion: If you buy canned fruit and vegetables, try to buy these items in glass or coated cans.

Comment: I prefer frozen vegetables over canned.

Peas and Potatoes with Cream Sauce

4 red potatoes
1 cup fresh or frozen peas
2 tablespoons butter
2 tablespoons unbleached flour
1/2 teaspoon sea salt
1/8 teaspoon white pepper
1 cup half and half

Cook potatoes. Add peas and let stand while preparing sauce. Melt butter, stir in flour, salt, and pepper. Add half and half. Bring to boil and cook for 1 minute. Drain potatoes and peas. Place in serving bowl and pour sauce over vegetables. Stir to coat.

Peas with Cashews

1 package frozen peas or 1 cup of fresh peas
1 cup chopped celery
1/2 cup minced sweet onion
1/4 cup mayonnaise
1/4 cup sour cream
1/2 teaspoon sea salt
1/2 cup cashews

Mix all ingredients together and sprinkle with snipped parsley.

Potatoes for Company

10 large potatoes, peeled and quartered
1 cup sour cream
1 (8 ounce) package cream cheese
1 stick butter
2 tablespoons minced sweet onion
1 teaspoon sea salt
1/2 teaspoon white pepper
Fresh snipped parsley

Cook and mash potatoes. Beat in sour cream, cream cheese, and butter. Add onion, salt, and pepper. Place in serving bowl and sprinkle with parsley.

Suggestion: This recipe can be placed in an ovenproof dish and placed in the oven until served.

Mashed Potatoes

2 pounds potatoes
1/4 cup butter
1/2 cup milk
1 teaspoon sea salt
1/4 teaspoon white pepper

Cook, drain, and mash potatoes. Mash in butter, milk, salt, and pepper.

Variation: Use buttermilk, potato water, and 1 teaspoon minced garlic.

Variation: Add chicken broth (homemade or with no MSG) to potatoes instead of milk.

Variation: Add a generous amount of powdered saffron to the milk and heat it before adding mixture to the mashed potatoes.

Variation: Add fresh chopped parsley, dill, or chives to mashed potatoes.

Variation: Cook equal amounts of potatoes and carrots and mash. Add sea salt, pepper, butter, and milk if needed.

Variation: Cook new potatoes with the skins on. Mash with skins, add butter, sea salt, and milk. Use an electric mixer instead of a potato masher.

Hint: To keep potatoes from browning, place peeled potatoes in salt water until all are potatoes have been peeled. You may also use water with a little vinegar.

Hint: Add a little unbleached sugar or fructose to older potatoes.

Hint: Add a little baking powder to mashed potatoes.

Hint: To keep potatoes white add a little vinegar to the water before cooking.

Potato Salad

3 pounds potatoes
4 boiled eggs, chopped
1/2 cup chopped sweet onion
1/2 cup chopped celery
1/2 cup sour cream
1 cup mayonnaise
1/4 cup sweet pickle juice
1/2 teaspoon dry mustard
1/2 teaspoon sea salt
1/4 teaspoon pepper

Cook potatoes in filtered water. Drain and let cool. Chop potatoes and add eggs, onion, and celery. Blend sour cream, mayonnaise, pickle juice, mustard, salt, and pepper.

Variation: Add 3 tablespoons apple cider vinegar or dill pickle juice and 2 tablespoons unbleached sugar in place of sweet pickle juice.

Variation: Add 1/2 pound snow peas and 1 can drained pitted black olives.

Suggestion: To save time peel, dice, and cook potatoes; Cool by setting the pan of drained potatoes in a bucket of ice cubes.

Sweet and Sour Cabbage

1/2 pound side pork or home smoked bacon
1 large onion
1 head white cabbage, shredded
1/4 cup apple cider vinegar
1/4 cup brown sugar
1 tablespoons sea salt
1/4 teaspoon pepper

Chop or grind side pork. Brown in a large skillet and remove some of the grease. Add onion and fry. Add shredded cabbage and fry until cabbage is wilted. Add vinegar, sugar, salt, and pepper. Add more sugar and vinegar to taste if necessary. Cook slowly for 2 hours.

Suggestion: You may have to fry some of the cabbage and transfer it to a larger kettle to cook. It will fry down to half the amount that you start with.

Sweet Potatoes (Baked)

4 sweet potatoes, peeled and cubed
1 sweet onion, chopped
1 teaspoon sea salt
Dash red pepper
1/2 cup butter
2 tablespoons pure maple syrup
1 tablespoons lemon juice
1 teaspoon cinnamon
Dash cumin
1/2 cup chopped pecans

Combine potatoes, onions, salt, and pepper. Melt butter in a shallow 11x7 inch baking dish and add potato mixture. Blend syrup, juice, cinnamon, and cumin. Pour over potato mixture. Sprinkle with pecans. Bake at 375° for 45 minutes.

Variation: Peel and cook sweet potatoes. Make syrup using 1/2 cup brown sugar, 1/4 cup butter, 3 tablespoons filtered water, and 1/2 teaspoon sea salt. Slice potatoes and arrange them in a baking dish. Pour the syrup over the potatoes. Bake for 20 minutes at 350°. Stir to coat.

Variation: Baked sweet potatoes may be served with butter, cinnamon, and brown sugar.

Sweet Onions and Green Beans

1 pound fresh green beans
Filtered water
1 large sweet onion
2 tablespoons butter
2 tablespoons raw sugar or unbleached
1/2 teaspoon sea salt
1/4 teaspoon pepper

Cook green beans in a little filtered water. Slice onions thin and fry in butter 5 minutes; do not stir. Cook for 10 minutes, stirring often. Cook until golden. Reduce to medium heat. Add sugar, salt, and pepper. Add green beans and cook for 5 minutes or until thoroughly heated.

Tasty Green Beans

1/2 cup chicken broth (homemade or with no MSG)
2 tablespoons soy sauce with no MSG
1/4 teaspoon unbleached sugar
1/2 teaspoon minced garlic
Pinch of ginger
1 pound green beans

Mix all ingredients together and cook until beans are tender.

Main Dishes

Casseroles

Asparagus Casserole

Beef Potato Casserole

Chicken Casserole with Noodles

Cauliflower Casserole

Baked Chicken Casserole

Cheesy Asparagus Casserole

Chicken Broccoli Casserole

Hash in the Oven

Potato Casserole

Scalloped Potatoes

Salmon Casserole

Asparagus Casserole

4 tablespoons butter
1 pound asparagus, cleaned
4 tablespoons unbleached flour
1 1/2 cups milk
1/2 cup cream
1/2 cup natural Cheddar cheese, shredded
1/2 cup natural white cheese, shredded
1 tablespoons Worcestershire sauce
1 teaspoon lemon juice
1/4 teaspoon sea salt
Dash pepper

Melt butter in casserole dish. Place asparagus in dish. Mix flour and a little of the milk. Add to remaining milk and cook over medium heat. Stir in cream, cheeses, Worcestershire sauce, lemon juice, salt, and pepper. Pour over the asparagus. Bake at 325° for 25 minutes.

Beef Potato Casserole

1 1/2 pound ground chuck
1/2 cup chopped onion
1/3 cup bread crumbs (from homemade bread)
3 tablespoons half and half
3/4 teaspoon sea salt
1/4 teaspoon pepper

Mix all ingredients and press into a 9-inch square pan. Bake at 350° for 30 minutes or until done. Top with peas, carrots, and potato cheese topping.

Potato Cheese Topping:
6 potatoes, cooked and mashed
1/2 stick butter
1/4 cup milk
1/2 teaspoon sea salt
1/4 teaspoon pepper
1/2 cup peas slightly cooked
1/2 cup carrots diced and cooked until tender
1/2 cup natural cheddar cheese, shredded

Cook and mash potatoes. Add butter, milk, salt, and pepper. Drain cooked peas and carrots. Arrange evenly on top of cooked meat. Spoon mashed potatoes on top and sprinkle potatoes with shredded cheese. Place in oven until served or microwave for 3 minutes. Cut into squares and serve. Serve with creamy cole slaw and biscuits.

Hint: Grate dried cheese and use in casserole dishes. Buttermilk will soften cheese. Use a warm knife to slice cheese. Cook cheese dishes slowly to keep them from curdling. This will prevent the cheese from becoming stringy.

Chicken Casserole with Noodles

2 cups cooked chicken, cubed
1 small onion, chopped
1/2 cup mayonnaise
2 tablespoons lemon juice
1/4 cup chopped sweet pepper
1/4 cup chopped red pepper
1/4 cup chopped yellow pepper
4 ounces natural jack cheese, shredded and divided
4 ounces natural Cheddar cheese, shredded and divided
1 cup chicken broth

Mix all ingredients. Add 1 teaspoon sea salt to 6 cups filtered water. Bring salt water to a boil and add 2 cups uncooked homemade noodles. Cook until tender. Drain. Add noodles to other ingredients. Mix well. Put into a baking dish. Bake at 350° for 30 minutes.

Cauliflower Casserole

1 head of cauliflower
2 cups medium white sauce
1/2 cup sour cream
1 cup natural sharp Cheddar cheese, shredded

Wash and cut cauliflower into bite size pieces. Combine medium white sauce, sour cream, and cheese. Bake at 350° for 20 minutes.

Medium White Sauce:
Melt 3 tablespoons butter and stir in 3 tablespoons unbleached flour. Gradually add 2 cups milk. Stir and cook until thick.

Baked Chicken Casserole

4 cups cooked, diced chicken
2 cups chopped celery
1 cup chopped carrots
½ cup slivered almonds
1 cup mayonnaise
1 cup milk or chicken broth
1 tablespoon unbleached flour
4 teaspoons lemon juice
1 small chopped onion
1 teaspoon sea salt
2 dashes pepper
2 cups natural Cheddar cheese, shredded

Mix all ingredients together and place in a baking dish. Top with fried bread crumbs.

Fried Bread Crumbs:
Melt butter in frying pan. Fry bread crumbs until light brown. Bake at 350° for 30 minutes.

Cheesy Asparagus Casserole

2 cups asparagus pieces
3 hard boiled eggs, chopped
1 cup natural sharp Cheddar cheese, shredded
Sprinkle of sea salt
Dash of pepper
½ cup bread crumbs
1 tablespoon butter
1 cup milk

Place asparagus in a 9-inch square baking dish. Scatter eggs and cheese on top of asparagus. Sprinkle with salt and pepper. Top with bread crumbs fried in butter. Add milk. Bake at 325° for 30 minutes.

Chicken Broccoli Casserole

6 chicken breasts
3 cup chopped broccoli
3/4 cup natural sharp Cheddar cheese
3 tablespoons unbleached flour
3 cups chicken broth
3/4 cup soft bread crumbs from homemade bread

Place chicken breasts on bottom of a baking dish. Add broccoli and cheese. Dissolve flour in a little of the chicken broth. Stir into the remaining broth and pour over the mixture in the baking dish. Top with breadcrumbs. Bake at 350° for 45 minutes or until done.

Hash in the Oven

1 cup cooked ground beef
1 cup chopped potatoes
1 chopped onion
1/4 cup snipped parsley
1 teaspoon sea salt
Dash of pepper
2 teaspoon Worcestershire sauce
2/3 cup half and half
1/2 cup bread crumbs
1 tablespoon butter

Mix first eight ingredients. Place in casserole dish. Brown bread crumbs in butter. Sprinkle on top of mixture in casserole dish. Bake at 350° for 30 minutes.

Potato Casserole

10 potatoes
1/4 cup butter, melted
2 cups chicken broth
2 tablespoons unbleached flour
2 cups sour cream
1/2 teaspoon sea salt
1/4 teaspoon pepper
1/2 cup chopped onion
2 cups natural Cheddar cheese, shredded
1/2 cup bread crumbs (homemade)

Cook potatoes until crisp tender. Cool and grate potatoes. Melt butter in broth. Dissolve the flour in a small amount of the broth and return to the pot. Cook until smooth. Blend in sour cream, salt, pepper, onion, and 1 1/2 cups cheese. Pour over potatoes and stir. Spoon into a buttered 9x13-inch baking dish. Bake at 350° uncovered for 30 minutes. Combine remaining cheese and bread crumbs. Sprinkle on top and bake 15 minutes.

Scalloped Potatoes

10 pound potatoes, peeled and sliced
1/2 cup shredded natural Cheddar cheese (optional)
1 sweet onion, peeled and sliced
3 tablespoons butter
1/2 cup unbleached flour
1 teaspoon sea salt
1/4 teaspoon pepper
2 cups milk

In a large baking dish layer potatoes, cheese, and onions; dab with butter and sprinkle with salt, pepper, and flour. Repeat. Pour milk over potato mixture. Bake at 350° for 1 hour. If you prefer, you can bake it for a longer time at a lower temperature.

Suggestion: To make cheese last longer, wipe with a vinegar soaked cloth and store in an airtight container.

Salmon Casserole

2 cups cooked salmon
1 small onion
Dash of pepper
1 or 2 drops hot sauce
½ cup bread crumbs (homemade)
1 egg

Combine all ingredients and bake at 350° for 30 minutes.

Main Dishes

Czechoslovakian Goulash

1 tablespoon lard
2 pounds stew beef, cubed
1 cup chopped celery
2 tablespoons paprika
1 cup chopped onions
1/4 cup snipped parsley
1 teaspoon sea salt
1/8 teaspoon pepper
2 quarts beef stock
1/4 cup pure cornstarch
1/4 cup filtered water

Melt lard in skillet and fry meat until tender and browned. Add celery, paprika, onions, parsley, salt, and pepper. Add beef broth from soup bones. Simmer for 2 hours. Dissolve cornstarch in water and pour into the meat and broth to thicken. Serve over noodles, mashed potatoes, or dumplings.

Variation: Add 2 cups diced tomatoes and 1 cup sour cream before thickening.

Cabbage Rolls with Meat

1/4 cup chopped onion
1/4 teaspoon pepper
1 teaspoon sea salt
1 egg
1 pound ground chuck
2 cups tomato juice
1/2 cup rice
Cabbage leaves
1 cup chopped tomatoes
1 cup filtered water

Combine onion, pepper, salt, egg, ground meat, tomato juice, and rice. Immerse cabbage head in water for 3 minutes to soften leaves. Separate leaves. Place 1/4 cup meat mixture on cabbage leaf. Roll up while folding in edge of leaf. Place in baking dish or small roaster. Add chopped tomatoes to the baking dish and 1 cup water. Bake at 350° for 1 hour. Broth may be thickened into gravy. Serve with mashed potatoes, noodles, or rice.

Variation: Mix 1 pound together beef and pork, 3/4 cup rice, and 1 teaspoon Worcestershire sauce. Follow directions above.

Baby Beef Liver Smothered in Onions

Wash and drain liver. Dredge in sea salt, black pepper, and unbleached flour. Heat 1/4 cup canola oil in a large skillet. Place liver in hot grease and fry fast on both sides. Slice a sweet onion on top of the liver; cover and let simmer for a few minutes. Remove liver and fry onions in drippings. Place onions on top of liver and serve.

Variation: Mushroom and Onion Sauce
Brown 4 tablespoons unbleached flour in 4 tablespoons butter. Add 1 1/2 cups chicken or beef broth, 1/2 cup filtered water, 1/2 teaspoon sea salt, and 1/4 teaspoon pepper. Cook and stir until thickened. Add 1 sweet onion, sliced and separated and 1 cup sliced mushrooms. Simmer for 5 minutes. Pour over fried liver. Try also on steak or roast beef.

Meatballs

¾ pound ground chuck
¾ pound ground pork
1½ cups crumbs from homemade bread
1 cup half and half
1 minced onion
1 tablespoon butter
1 egg
¼ cup snipped parsley
1¼ teaspoons sea salt
Dash of pepper
Pinch of ginger
2 tablespoons butter for frying meatballs
2 tablespoons butter for gravy
2 tablespoons unbleached flour
3 tablespoons filtered water
1 cup beef broth or 1 cup coffee

Mix meats together. Soak bread crumbs in half and half. Cook onion in butter. Combine meats, crumb mixture, onion, egg, parsley, salt, pepper, and ginger. Beat 2 minutes with electric mixer. Chill in refrigerator for 2 hours. Shape into 1½-inch balls. Brown meatballs in butter.

To serve with gravy remove meatballs from skillet. Add 2 tablespoons butter to drippings. Dissolve flour in water. Add to drippings with beef broth. Cook until thick. Add meatballs and simmer for 30 minutes. Serve with mashed potatoes or over noodles.

Cocktail Meatballs

Heat equal amounts of homemade pizza sauce and grape jelly. Add meatballs to the sauce, coating them. Simmer for 30 minutes.

Suggestion: Use store bought pizza or spaghetti sauce if it is all natural.

Meatloaf

1 1/2 cups bread crumbs (homemade)
1 celery rib, chopped
1 small onion, chopped
1 clove garlic, pressed
1/4 cup parsley, snipped
1/2 cup catsup (homemade is best if you have it)
1 tablespoons mustard
1/2 pound ground pork
1/2 pound ground chuck
1/2 pound ground veal
2 eggs
2 teaspoons sea salt
1/2 teaspoon pepper
1 cup tomato sauce
1/4 cup catsup for topping
2 tablespoons brown sugar
Onion slices

Combine all but the last three items. Place into a baking dish and shape into a log. Mix brown sugar and catsup together and pour over meat. Arrange onion slices on top. Bake at 375° for 1 hour (160° on meat thermometer).

Suggestion: Grease or butter dish before adding meat loaf to eliminate sticking.

Pioneer Stew

2 pounds round steak, cubed
2 tablespoons lard
4 cups filtered water
2 onions, sliced
2 teaspoons sea salt
1/4 teaspoon pepper
1/2 teaspoon paprika
3 cups sliced carrots
4 cups diced potatoes
2 cups chopped tomatoes
2 tablespoons snipped parsley
1/2 cup fresh peas or frozen
1 tablespoons molasses
1/4 cup unbleached flour
1/2 cup filtered water

Heat lard in a dutch oven and brown the meat. Add 4 cups water, onions, salt, pepper, and paprika. Bring to boil and reduce heat. Cover and simmer for 1 1/2 hours. Add carrots, potatoes, tomatoes, and parsley. Cover and simmer until vegetables are tender. Stir in peas and molasses. Dissolve flour in 1/2 water and add to the stew. Cook for 10 minutes.

Variation: Add 1/2 cup pearl barley to the stew. Allow to simmer for 2 hours.

Beef Stroganoff

2 tablespoons canola oil
1/2 pound round steak, sliced
1/4 cup sweet onion, chopped
1/2 cup mushrooms
2 cloves garlic, pressed
1/2 cup beef broth (homemade or with no MSG)
1 tablespoons Worcestershire sauce
1/4 teaspoon dry mustard
1 tablespoons unbleached flour
1 teaspoon butter, softened
2 tablespoons sour cream

Fry beef slices in oil. Cook until tender. Add onions, mushrooms, garlic, broth, Worcestershire sauce, and mustard. Cream flour and butter together; stir into hot mixture. Cook and stir until thick. Add sour cream. Serve over homemade noodles.

Homemade Noodles:
Mix 1 cup unbleached flour, 1 egg and 2 tablespoons milk. Knead on floured board until stiff and dough does not stick to your hands. Roll out until dough is thin. Let set for 10 minutes. Roll up and cut into 1/8 inch strips. Cook in boiling filtered water for 15 minutes or until tender.

Pot Roast

3 pound rump roast, chuck or shoulder
1 teaspoon sea salt
1/8 teaspoon pepper
Unbleached flour
1/4 cup lard
1/2 cup filtered water
1 onion, chopped
1 tablespoon snipped parsley
1/4 cup unbleached flour for gravy
1/2 cup filtered water for gravy

Rub roast with salt, pepper, and flour. Melt lard in a dutch oven. Add meat and cook until brown on both sides. Add water, onion, and parsley. Cover; cook slowly for 4 hours or until tender. Dissolve flour in water and thicken broth. Serve with dumplings, homemade noodles, or mashed potatoes.

Variation: Add 1 cup tomato juice or chopped tomatoes. Thicken as you would other gravies.

Hint: To help tenderize a beef roast, add 1 tablespoon of apple cider vinegar.

Hint: If you are using venison or other wild meat soak meat in vinegar water for an hour before cooking. Use 1/4 cup apple cider vinegar to 1 quart of filtered water.

Rolled Rump Roast

Rub meat with sea salt and black pepper. Using a shaker with 6 parts sea salt and 1 part pepper works great. Allow 42 minutes per pound at 260°. Serve with horse radish sauce.

Horseradish Sauce:
Whip 1/2 cup cream, pinch of sea salt, 1 tablespoon lemon juice, and 1/4 cup horseradish.

Standing Roast

Rub meat with sea salt and black pepper. Slow roast at 260°. Allow 24 minutes per pound. At 135° on meat thermometer meat will be medium rare. At 160° meat will be done. Serve with mushroom sauce.

Mushroom Sauce:
Brown 4 tablespoons unbleached flour in 4 tablespoons butter. Add 1 1/2 cups chicken or beef broth, 1/2 cup filtered water, 1/2 teaspoon sea salt, and 1/4 teaspoon pepper. Add 1 cup sliced mushrooms and simmer for 2 minutes.

Filet Mignon

Remove skin and fat from tenderloin. Rub both sides with olive oil. Place in baking dish. Cover with strips of salt pork. Bake in a hot oven 450° for 15 minutes. Lower temperature to 350° and bake 20 minutes. Serve with sour cream mustard sauce.

Sour Cream Mustard Sauce:
Combine 1 1/4 cups sour cream, 2 tablespoons mustard, 1 teaspoon sea salt, 1/4 teaspoon pepper and 3 tablespoons lemon juice.

Grilled T-Bone Steak

Marinate 2 pounds steak in 1/2 cup Worcestershire sauce, 1 tablespoon fine chopped onion, 2 tablespoons olive oil, 2 tablespoons apple cider vinegar, 1 teaspoon peppercorns and 1 teaspoon sea salt. Seal in a plastic bag. Place in refrigerator for 1 hour. Turn over every 15 minutes. Grill and use extra marinade to baste.

Suggestion: Use kiwi fruit or papaya (seeds and pulp) to tenderize steaks. Marinade for 20 minutes. Do not leave on meat for too long.

Salisbury Steak

1 1/2 pound ground chuck
1/2 cup homemade bread crumbs
1 egg
1/4 teaspoon sea salt
1/4 teaspoon white pepper
1 tablespoon canola oil
1 tablespoon unbleached flour
1/4 cup filtered water
1/4 cup catsup
1 teaspoon Worcestershire sauce
1/2 teaspoon mustard

Combine meat, crumbs, egg, salt, and pepper. Shape into 6 patties. Heat oil in skillet. Brown patties. Remove from skillet. Discard excess oil. Dissolve flour in water. Pour into skillet with catsup, Worcestershire sauce, and mustard. Cook 2 minutes. Return patties to skillet. Cover and simmer 20 minutes. Serve over homemade noodles or mashed potatoes.

Swiss Steak

Select round steak, shoulder, or chuck steak. Rub meat with sea salt and pepper. Dust with unbleached flour. Pound flour into steak. Sear in olive oil. Slice onion and place on top of meat. Add 1/2 cup filtered water. Cover and simmer until meat is done. Remove meat. Thicken gravy with 1/4 cup unbleached flour and 1/2 cup filtered water. Add extra water if needed. Serve with mashed potatoes.

Variation: Prepare steak. Add 1 cup filtered water, 1 cup tomatoes, 1 cup sour cream. Cook. Add 1/2 cup filtered water when meat is done. Simmer for 1/2 hour. Thicken. Serve with dumplings.

Baked Chicken

Chicken pieces
1/4 cup lemon juice
Sprinkle of sea salt
Sprinkle of pepper
1/2 cup unbleached flour
1/4 cup lard
2 tablespoons brown sugar
1 lemon slice
1 1/4 cups chicken broth (homemade or with no MSG)

Baste chicken with lemon juice. Sprinkle with salt and pepper. Dredge in flour. Melt lard in skillet and brown chicken. Transfer chicken to baking dish. Combine sugar, lemon slice, and broth. Pour over chicken. Bake at 350° for 40 minutes or until done.

Baked Chicken Breast

4 tablespoons mustard
2 tablespoons filtered water
1 teaspoon garlic powder
1/2 teaspoon all natural Italian dressing (homemade)
1 pound boneless chicken breasts

Mix all ingredients together and marinate in a sealed plastic bag for 1 hour. Turn occasionally. Place in buttered baking dish. Bake at 375° for 20 minutes or until done. Serve with herb butter dip.

Herb Butter Dip:
1/2 pound butter
1 tablespoon cilantro, chopped
1 tablespoon parsley, chopped
1 tablespoon basil
1/4 teaspoon sea salt or seasoned salt
Dash of pepper

Chicken (Deep Fried)

Sprinkle fryer size chicken pieces with sea salt and pepper. Fry in hot grease (380°) for 6 to 7 minutes.

Chicken (Fried with Flour)

Rub sea salt and pepper on chicken pieces. Shake in plastic bag with unbleached flour. Melt 1/4 cup lard and 1/4 cup butter in a skillet and fry chicken on medium heat, turning often, until browned. Cover and let simmer until done. Approximately 45 minutes.

Chicken (Fried without Flour)

Wash and drain chicken pieces. Melt 1 stick of butter in skillet on medium heat. Place chicken in skillet. Fry, turning often, for about 45 minutes. Partially cover and turn heat to low setting for 10 minutes or until done. It is not necessary to salt chicken if using salted butter. Add pepper if desire.

Honey Mustard Chicken

4 boneless, skinless chicken breasts
1 cup homemade bread crumbs
1 tablespoon dry mustard
3 tablespoons honey
1 tablespoon mustard (prepared)
Butter for frying

Mix 1 cup bread crumbs and 1 tablespoons dry mustard. Mix well and set aside. Combine 3 tablespoons honey and 1 tablespoons mustard. Mix well and dredge chicken in the honey mustard mixture then coat with bread crumb mixture. Melt butter in frying pan. Place chicken in pan and fry on both sides until done. Serve with honey mustard butter sauce.

Honey Mustard Butter Sauce:
Melt 3/4 cup butter. Stir in 1 cup honey and 1/4 to 1/2 cup mustard until dissolved. Adjust portions to taste.

Lemon Glazed Chicken Breast

2 tablespoons butter
4 chicken breasts, boned and skinned
1/2 teaspoon sea salt
1 tablespoon lemon juice
1/2 lemon, sliced thin
2 tablespoons minced sweet onion
1 tablespoon pure cornstarch
1/2 cup chicken broth (homemade or with no MSG)

Melt butter in skillet. Fry chicken until brown on both sides. Add salt and lemon juice. Place lemon slices and minced onion on chicken. Bring to a boil. Cover and simmer until chicken is done. Remove chicken. Dissolve cornstarch in broth. Stir into skillet. Simmer 3 minutes. Pour over chicken and serve. If you do not have chicken broth use lemon sauce recipe below.

Variation: Lemon Sauce:
1 tablespoon butter
1 tablespoons unbleached flour
1/4 teaspoon sea salt
1/8 teaspoon white pepper
1/2 cup milk
1/2 teaspoon lemon juice
1/2 teaspoon grated lemon rind

Combine all ingredients and cook for 1 minute. Serve over cooked chicken breast.

Chicken Paprika

5 pounds chicken, fryer size
2 teaspoon sea salt
2 teaspoon paprika
1/2 cup butter
1 sweet onion
1 teaspoon paprika
2 cups filtered water
1 pint sour cream
3/4 cup filtered water
1/4 cup unbleached flour

Sprinkle chicken parts with salt and paprika. Melt butter in frying pan. Add chicken. Fry until golden on both sides. Add onion and sprinkle with 1 teaspoon paprika. Cover and simmer for 20 minutes. Add 2 cups water. Cook slowly, covered, until tender. Remove chicken. Mix sour cream, 3/4 cup water, and 1/4 cup flour. Stir until smooth. Gradually add to broth in skillet. Return chicken to skillet. Simmer until serving time. Serve with dumplings.

Dumplings:
Combine 4 cups unbleached flour, 2 teaspoons baking powder, 1 cup milk, 4 eggs and 2 teaspoons sea salt. Mix well. Drop by spoonfuls into a large kettle of boiling filtered water.

Hint: For an easy release dip spoon into hot water before dipping into dough. Cover and boil 5 minutes, uncover and boil 5 more minutes. Drain in a colander. Sprinkle lightly with paprika.

Honey Orange Glazed Duck

1 cup pure orange juice
1/4 cup honey
1/4 cup mustard
2 tablespoons lemon juice
Pinch of red pepper
1/4 teaspoon chili powder
1/4 teaspoon nutmeg
1/4 fresh ground pepper
1/2 teaspoon sea salt
Sea salt and pepper for sprinkling

Select two muscovy ducks. Wash and sprinkle with salt and pepper. Place in roaster. Mix all ingredients and cook 1 minute. Pour 1/2 of the glaze over the ducks. Bake at 275° for 4 hours. Remove from oven. Sprinkle with more salt and pepper. Grill until thermometer reaches 160°. Baste with remaining orange glaze.

Roast Turkey

Select a 12 pound turkey. If turkey is frozen thaw in refrigerator for two days prior to cooking. Be sure to remove giblets. Wash and dry bird. Rub sea salt and pepper inside the cavity then salt the outer skin. Slice 1 orange and place in the cavity of the bird. Make a bouquet from sprigs of rosemary, parsley, green onions, and celery leaves. Tie with a cord and place in the cavity with orange slices.

Place in roaster or in a roasting bag. If using a roasting bag, the turkey will get done much sooner. If using a roaster bake at 325° for 4 hours or until thermometer reaches 180°. Bird is done when leg easily pulls away from the body. Place turkey on cutting board. Discard bouquet and orange slices in cavity.

Horseradish Giblet Gravy:
Place giblets, neck, and wing tips in a pot with 2 1/2 cups filtered water. Add a little celery, onion, 1 teaspoon sea salt and a dash of white pepper. Cook 1 hour or until meat can be removed from the bone and giblets can be cut up in small pieces. Return meat to pot. Add all drippings and broth from the turkey. Thicken broth. Add 1 tablespoon horseradish. Serve over mashed potatoes.

Bread Stuffing:
Combine 6 cups homemade dried bread cubes, 2 teaspoons snipped parsley, 1/2 stick melted butter, 1 teaspoon sea salt, 1/4 teaspoon pepper, 1 1/2 teaspoons sage, 6 teaspoons poultry seasoning, 2 ribs celery (chopped), 1 small onion (chopped), 3 eggs, and enough filtered water or broth to moisten well. Place in baking dish and bake at 350° for 1 hour. It is not recommended to place stuffing inside cavity of bird.

Pineapple B-B-Q Ribs

4 pounds country style ribs, browned
Filtered water for cooking
1 teaspoon sea salt
1 1/2 cups pineapple, chopped
2 cans tomato sauce
1/2 cup chopped sweet onion
1/2 cup chopped sweet red pepper
1 cup brown sugar
1/4 cup apple cider vinegar
1/4 cup tomato paste
1/2 cup filtered water
2 tablespoons Worcestershire sauce
1 clove garlic, pressed
1/4 teaspoon pepper

Cook ribs in filtered water, with 1 teaspoon sea salt, for 35 minutes. Place ribs in shallow pan. Combine ingredients and bake at 350° for 2 1/2 hours or until done.

If you prefer, bake at 300° for 6 to 8 hours.

Pork Chops (Breaded)

Sprinkle pork chops with sea salt and fresh ground pepper. Beat egg and a little milk and dip chops into the mixture. Roll in finely grated homemade breadcrumbs. Heat 1 tablespoon of lard or canola oil in a skillet. Brown chops on both sides. Place in a baking dish. Bake at 350° for 45 minutes or until tender.

Pork Loin Chops (Grilled)

Select 6 loin chops. Place in a tightly sealed bag with 1/4 cup Worcestershire sauce, 2 teaspoons sea salt, and 1 teaspoon fresh ground pepper. Marinate for 2 hours. Grill.

Pork Chops with Dry Rub

Sprinkle pork chops with dry rub seasoning salt. Place on a lightly greased rack in a broiler pan. Bake at 325° for 45 minutes.

Dry Rub Seasoning Salt:
1 cup sea salt
2 teaspoons dry mustard
1 1/2 teaspoons dried oregano
1 teaspoon dried marjoram
1 teaspoon dried thyme
1 teaspoon garlic powder
1 teaspoon curry powder
1/2 teaspoon celery salt
1/4 teaspoon dried dill weed
1/2 teaspoon powdered saffron

Combine all ingredients. Use on vegetables, meats, and salads. Store unused portion in an airtight container in the refrigerator.

Pork Chops and Onion Gravy

4 pork chops
1/2 teaspoon sea salt
1/4 teaspoon pepper
2 tablespoons unbleached flour
2 teaspoon olive oil
1 large sliced sweet onion
1 cup chicken or beef broth (homemade or with no MSG)
1 teaspoon pure cornstarch or unbleached flour
2 tablespoon filtered water to dissolve cornstarch

Mix salt, pepper, and flour. Coat pork chops with mixture. Heat oil in skillet. Add pork chops and fry 3 minutes on each side. Add onion slices. Cook 5 minutes. Add broth and simmer until tender. Remove and place on serving platter. Dissolve cornstarch or flour in water. Pour into onions and drippings. Cook slightly and pour over the pork chops.

Hint: If you prefer a darker gravy place brown onion skins in the gravy while cooking; remove them before serving.

Pork Chops (Stuffed)

Choose 1 inch thick, boneless, pork chops. Slice to within 1/2 inch of the edge. Open pork chop and sprinkle with sea salt and pepper. Fill each pork chop with 1/2 cup stuffing. Close and tie with cord. Heat 2 tablespoons olive oil in a skillet. Brown the chops. Turn over once and brown. Transfer pork chops to baking dish. Bake at 375° for 30 minutes.

Stuffing:
Cube and dry 1 loaf (homemade) bread. Add 1/4 cup melted butter, 2 diced celery ribs, 1/2 cup chopped sweet onion, 1 pint chicken broth, and 1 tablespoons sage. Mix well.

Pork Loin with Sour Cream Gravy

3 1/2 pound pork loin
1/4 cup butter
1/4 cup snipped fresh parsley
1 teaspoon sea salt
Pepper
1 sweet onion quartered
8 carrots
1 cup chicken broth (homemade or with no MSG)
2 tablespoons unbleached flour
1/2 cup sour cream
Filtered water for gravy

Melt butter in a skillet and sear roast all around. Place in a shallow baking dish. Sprinkle with parsley, salt, and pepper. Add onions, carrots, and chicken broth. Bake at 350° for 3 hours or until meat thermometer registers 165°. Pour drippings into a large saucepan. Add enough water to measure 3 cups. Place flour and sour cream in a saucepan with drippings and water. Cook and stir until thick. Serve over mashed potatoes.

Hint: Add a pinch of sea salt to the flour before adding to the broth. This will make gravy smoother.

Hint: Add 1 teaspoon baking soda to high fat gravy.

Pork Sausage Gravy

3/4 pound ground pork, without seasonings (seasoned pork may contain MSG)
1 teaspoon sea salt
2 teaspoon brown sugar
1/2 teaspoon pepper
1 tablespoon sage
1/4 cup unbleached flour
1 cup milk
1 cup half and half
Dash of red pepper (optional)

Mix pork, salt, pepper, and sage. Brown in a skillet. Remove sausage with a slotted spoon. Pour drippings in a glass measuring cup. Dip off clear lard when it settles (save lard for other uses like pie crusts, biscuits, or to fry eggs). Use 1/3 cup bottom drippings for gravy. Return the 1/3 cup drippings to the skillet. Sprinkle 1/4 cup flour over the drippings. Cook and stir into drippings for 3 minutes or until lightly browned. Add cooked sausage. Stir while adding milk and half and half. Cook and stir until thick. Add dash of red pepper if desired. Serve over biscuits.

Hint: Add 1/4 cup coffee to gravy to make it go further.

Hint: If you burn the gravy add a teaspoon of peanut butter.

Sausage Patties (Fresh)

Mix 1 pound fresh ground, unseasoned pork with 1/2 teaspoon sage, 1/2 teaspoon sea salt, and fresh ground pepper. Form into patties and fry until juice runs clear.

Raisin Sauce with Home Smoked Ham

1 home smoked ham
2 cups filtered water
4 cups chicken broth (homemade or with no MSG)
1 1/2 cups cranberry juice
1 cup pure orange juice
2/3 cup gold raisins
2/3 cup dark raisins
1 tablespoon whole cloves
1 tablespoon pure cornstarch
Filtered water to dissolve cornstarch

Place ham in baking dish. Add water and bake for 2 hours at 350°. Remove ham. Add chicken broth, juices, raisins, and cloves to ham broth. Dissolve cornstarch in a little water and add to other ingredients. Simmer sauce while you slice the ham. Serve raisin sauce over the ham or on the side.

Comment: Cloves may be placed in a tea container or cheesecloth and removed if you do not want them in the sauce.

Comment: Some meat lockers or slaughter houses will make smoked hams and bacon for you without the nitrites.

Main Dishes

Oriental Food

Beef Strip Stir-Fry

Chicken in Garlic Sauce

Hoisin Sauce with Shrimp

Orange Pepper Chicken

Oriental Stir-Fry

Sesame Chicken

Shrimp with Garlic Sauce

Shrimp with Pea Pods

Sweet and Sour Shrimp

Sweet and Sour Shrimp (battered)

Beef Strip Stir-Fry

1 tablespoon Worcestershire sauce
1 tablespoon soy sauce with no MSG
4 tablespoons apple cider vinegar
1 clove garlic, pressed
1/2 teaspoon ginger
1 teaspoon unbleached sugar
1/2 pound sirloin steak, cut in strips
1/2 cup broccoli, cut up
1/2 cup cauliflower, cut up
1/2 cup olive oil
1/4 cup diced red peppers
1/4 cup diced green peppers
1/2 cup chopped sweet onion
1 tablespoon pure cornstarch
3 tablespoons beef or chicken broth (homemade or with no MSG)

Combine sauces, vinegar, garlic, sugar, and steak strips. Place in a tightly sealed bag and marinate in refrigerator for 1 hour. Stir fry broccoli and cauliflower in oil until softened. Add beef and the marinade. Cook for 3 minutes. Add peppers and onions. Stir-fry for 3 minutes. Combine cornstarch and broth. Add to stir fry and cook for 2 minutes. Serve over rice or noodles.

Comment: Canned broth can be used if it does not contain MSG. It is available in some stores.

Chicken in Garlic Sauce

1/2 cup chicken broth (homemade or with No MSG)
1 1/2 teaspoons pure cornstarch
2 tablespoons butter
1/2 red pepper, cut in strips
1/2 green pepper, cut in strips
1/2 cup sweet onion, chopped
1 carrot sliced thin
3 teaspoons minced garlic
1 tablespoon butter for frying
1 pound chicken breast, sliced into thin strips
1/4 teaspoon sea salt
2 tablespoons snipped parsley

Combine broth and cornstarch and set aside. Melt butter in a wok. Stir fry peppers, onions, carrots, and garlic for 3 minutes. Remove vegetables. Add 1 tablespoon butter and chicken. Stir fry over medium high heat for 5 minutes or until chicken is cooked. Push meat from center of wok. Pour sauce into the center of the wok. Stir-fry until thick. Return vegetables to wok. Add salt and parsley. Stir until all ingredients are coated. Serve over rice.

Suggestion: Store garlic in a jar of olive oil and keep in refrigerator.

Hoisin Sauce with Shrimp

2 tablespoons hoisin sauce (with no MSG)
1 tablespoon apple cider vinegar
2 teaspoons unbleached sugar
1/2 teaspoon sea salt
3 tablespoons peanut oil
1 teaspoon grated fresh ginger
1 tablespoon minced sweet onion

Mix and use in stir frying shrimp, chicken, fish, beef, pork, or vegetables.

For 1 pound cleaned shrimp heat oil in wok for 2 minutes. Stir fry shrimp 5 minutes or until pink. Add hoisin sauce. Stir until well coated.

Orange Pepper Chicken

3 pounds chicken pieces
2 tablespoons olive oil
1 sweet onion, sliced
1/2 sweet red pepper, cut in strips
1/2 sweet green pepper, cut in strips
4 cloves of garlic, pressed
1 cup pure orange juice
1 teaspoon grated orange zest (peel)
1 teaspoon sea salt
1/2 teaspoon white pepper
1/2 cup chicken broth (homemade or with no MSG)
2 tablespoons pure cornstarch
3 tablespoons filtered water

Brown chicken in oil. Remove and set aside. Sauté onion, peppers, and garlic. Return chicken to pan. Add orange juice, zest, salt, pepper, and broth. Bring to a boil and reduce heat. Cover and simmer for 40 minutes. Transfer chicken to serving platter. Dissolve cornstarch in water and thicken broth. Serve over rice.

Oriental Stir Fry

2/3 cup cauliflower
1/2 cup sliced carrots
2/3 cup broccoli
2/3 cup pea pods
1/2 sweet onion, chopped
1/2 cup chopped red pepper
1/2 cup chopped green pepper
1/2 cup pineapple
1/4 cup peanut oil

Stir fry vegetables and raw pineapple in wok or frying pan. Use peanut oil or olive oil. Stir fry until crisp tender. Add oriental sauce and serve.

Oriental Sauce:
2 tablespoons pure cornstarch
3/4 cup chicken broth (homemade or with no MSG)
3/4 cup brown sugar
3 tablespoons molasses
1 cup apple cider vinegar
1/4 cup pineapple juice
Mix well. Use in stir fry.

Sesame Chicken

1 1/2 pounds skinless, boneless chicken breast
1/2 cup unbleached flour
1 1/2 teaspoons lemon pepper
3/4 teaspoon sea salt
1/3 cup sesame seeds
2 teaspoons virgin olive oil
2 cups sliced mushrooms
1/4 cup chopped sweet onion
2 tablespoons unbleached flour
1 1/2 cups milk
1 tablespoon snipped parsley
1 tablespoon dry mustard
1/3 cup milk
1 tablespoon virgin olive oil
1 teaspoon toasted sesame oil

Wash and drain chicken. Set aside. Blend flour, lemon pepper, salt, and sesame seeds. Set aside. Heat 2 teaspoons oil in a skillet. Cook mushrooms and onions until tender. Stir 2 tablespoons flour into mushroom mixture until blended. Add 1 1/2 cups milk. Cook until mixture is bubbly and thick. Stir in parsley and mustard. Keep warm. Dip chicken in 1/3 cup milk, and roll in flour-sesame mixture. Add 1 tablespoon olive oil and 1 tablespoon sesame oil to skillet. Cook chicken on both sides until done. Serve with sweet and sour apricot sauce:

Sweet and Sour Apricot Sauce:
Cook 1 cup pitted apricots, 1 cup filtered water, and 1 cup unbleached sugar. Sieve apricots. Add 1/2 cup mayonnaise, 1/2 cup catsup, 1/4 cup soy sauce, 1 teaspoon ginger and 1 teaspoon lemon juice.

Serve mushroom onion mixture over rice. Use Sweet and Sour Apricot Sauce for dipping chicken.

Shrimp with Garlic Sauce

1 1/2 cups rice
1 1/2 cups filtered water
1/4 teaspoon sea salt
1/2 cup chicken broth (with no MSG)
1 1/2 teaspoons pure cornstarch
1/2 medium red pepper, cut into strips
1/2 medium green pepper, cut into strips
Thin slices of carrot
1/2 cup sweet onion, cut up
2 teaspoons minced garlic
2 tablespoons butter
1 (12 ounce) package frozen shrimp, peeled and deveined
2 tablespoons snipped fresh parsley

Cook rice with filtered water and salt. Set aside. Combine broth and corn starch and set aside. Place 1 tablespoon butter in wok; cook peppers, carrot, onions, and garlic over medium high heat for three minutes. Remove vegetables. Place shrimp and remaining butter in the wok. Stir fry over medium high heat 3 minutes or until shrimp turn pink. Push shrimp from center of wok. Stir sauce and pour into the center of the wok. Cook and stir until thick. Return vegetables to wok and stir until coated with sauce. Cook and stir 1 minute and serve over rice.

Shrimp with Pea Pods

2 1/2 cups chicken broth (with no MSG)
3 pound shrimp, peeled and deveined
1/2 cup chopped sweet onion
3 tablespoons soy sauce (with no MSG)
1 teaspoon sea salt
4 tablespoons pure cornstarch
1/4 cup filtered water
1 cup mushrooms
1 pound Chinese pea pods, cleaned and washed

Heat chicken broth. Add shrimp, onions, soy sauce, and salt. Cook uncovered for 3 minutes. Stir occasionally. Dissolve cornstarch in 1/4 cup water. Stir into shrimp mixture. Cook until thick. Add mushrooms and pea pods. Cook for 3 minutes. Serve.

Sweet and Sour Shrimp

1 pound cleaned deveined shrimp

Marinade:
Mix 1/3 cup cornstarch, 1 tablespoon cranberry juice, 1 tablespoon soy sauce (with no MSG). Add shrimp and stir to coat. Set aside.

Main ingredients:
Heat 1 tablespoon canola oil; slice and stir fry 1/2 green pepper, 1/2 red pepper, and 1/2 sweet onion for 2 minutes. Drain 1 1/2 cups pineapple chunks; reserve juice. While making sweet and sour sauce, fry shrimp in 2 cups canola oil in a wok.

Sweet and Sour Sauce:
Combine 1 tablespoons pure cornstarch, 3 tablespoons unbleached sugar, 1/2 cup orange or pineapple juice, 1/4 cup apple cider vinegar, 1/4 cup catsup, 1 1/2 teaspoons (MSG free) soy sauce, and 2 cloves pressed garlic. Cook for 2 minutes. Add pineapple, peppers, onions, and shrimp. Toss lightly and heat briefly. Serve over cooked rice.

Sweet and Sour Shrimp (Battered)

1 1/2 pound cleaned and peeled shrimp
Canola oil (enough to fry shrimp)
2 eggs
1/2 teaspoon baking powder
1/4 teaspoon sea salt
1/2 cup unbleached flour
1 green pepper, cut into strips
1 1/2 cups golden ripe pineapple (save all juice)
1/2 cup apple cider vinegar
2/3 cup unbleached sugar
1/2 teaspoon sea salt
1 tablespoons soy sauce
1/2 cup filtered water
1 1/2 tablespoons cornstarch

Heat 1 1/2 inches of oil to 375°, in a 2 1/2-inch deep fry frying pan or dutch oven. While oil is heating blend eggs, baking powder, salt, and flour into a batter. Add shrimp and coat evenly. Fry in oil until golden. Remove to hot plate to keep warm. Empty all but 2 tablespoons oil from frying pan. Lightly fry peppers and add pineapple with the juice, vinegar, sugar, salt, and soy sauce. Cook 6 minutes, stirring constantly. Dissolve cornstarch in water and pour into frying pan. Cook until thick. Stir in shrimp or scallops. Serve with basmati rice.

Hot Mustard Sauce:
1 egg
1/4 cup brown sugar
3 tablespoons unbleached sugar
1 teaspoon mustard
Dash hot sauce
Mix all ingredients and cook until thick. Use in any Chinese dish.

Main Dishes

Pastas/Sauces/Pizza

Lasagna

Veggie Lasagna

Macaroni and Cheese (Baked)

Macaroni Chicken and Cheese

Egg Noodles and Pasta, Spaetzle

Alfredo Sauce, Pizza/Spaghetti Sauce

Pizza Dough

Veggie Pizza

Lasagna

Lasagna noodles (homemade or all natural from store)
1 pound ground chuck
1 chopped sweet onion
2 cloves garlic, pressed
2 cups chopped tomatoes
1 cup pizza sauce (homemade) or tomato sauce
1 tablespoon minced parsley
1 tablespoon unbleached sugar
2 teaspoon sea salt
1 teaspoon basil
1 teaspoon paprika
1 teaspoon oregano
½ pound white natural jack cheese
½ pound natural mozzarella cheese
1 cup sour cream
⅓ cup grated Parmesan
Feta cheese

Cook noodles. Place a layer in a 9x13-inch baking dish. Fry beef and onion until browned. Combine meat, garlic, tomatoes, sauce, parsley, sugar, salt, basil, paprika, and oregano. Spoon half of the mixture onto cooked noodles in baking dish. Shred jack and mozzarella cheese and mix with sour cream. Spoon half of the cheese mixture over the sauce and noodles. Sprinkle with Parmesan cheese. Crumble half of the feta cheese on top. Place a layer of noodles on top and repeat with meat sauce and cheese mixture. Sprinkle with Parmesan. Add remaining feta cheese. Place a layer of noodles of top and bake at 350° for 1 hour. Bake on lower rack and place a foil on the top rack to keep from drying out.

Note: All natural pastas may be found in a special section at most supermarkets.

Veggie Lasagna

2 small zucchini
1/2 bunch broccoli
2 cups chopped spinach
2 tablespoons butter
1/4 teaspoon sea salt
Lasagna noodles (homemade all natural also available at store)
3 tablespoons butter
1/4 unbleached flour
2 1/2 cups milk
1/4 cup Parmesan cheese
2 eggs
15 ounce package ricotta cheese
8 ounces mozzarella

Chop zucchini, broccoli, and spinach. Cook in 2 tablespoons butter and 1/4 teaspoon salt. Cook and stir until vegetables are done. Cook noodles. Place a layer of the noodles in a 9x13-inch baking dish. Melt 3 tablespoons butter. Add flour. Gradually add milk. Cook and stir until sauce boils and thickens. Remove from heat and stir in the Parmesan cheese. Mix together eggs and ricotta cheese. Spoon 1/2 of the cheese mixture and 1/2 of the vegetables on the noodles and sprinkle with half of the mozzarella. Place noodles on top and repeat with the other half. Bake at 350° for 45 minutes.

Macaroni and Cheese (Baked)

2 cups cooked macaroni (homemade or all natural)
1 cup shredded natural Cheddar cheese
1 1/2 cups milk
2 eggs
1/4 cup minced onion
1/2 teaspoon sea salt
1/4 teaspoon white pepper
1/4 cup chopped green pepper
1/4 cup minced sweet red pepper
1 tablespoon butter
1/2 cup homemade bread crumbs

Mix macaroni, shredded Cheddar, milk, eggs, onion, sea salt, white pepper, and sweet peppers. Pour into well greased baking dish. Melt butter and fry bread crumbs until lightly browned. Scatter on top of the macaroni mixture. Bake at 375° for 45 minutes.

Suggestion: Serve garlic toast with any pasta dish.

Garlic Toast:
Melt 1 stick butter in a saucepan and add 1 teaspoon minced garlic. Heat frying pan or grill. Spoon butter and garlic mixture on both sides of a slice of homemade bread and place in a frying pan or on grill. Brown both sides and serve.

Macaroni Chicken and Cheese

2 cups all natural uncooked macaroni (or homemade)
4 cups chicken broth or 2 cups broth and 2 cups filtered water
2 cups cooked, cubed chicken
1/2 cup natural jack cheese, shredded
1/2 cup natural Cheddar cheese, shredded
2 ounces cream cheese
2 tablespoons Parmesan cheese
1/3 cup milk
1/2 teaspoon sea salt
1/4 teaspoon white pepper
2 teaspoons fresh snipped parsley

Cook macaroni in chicken broth. Add chicken. Melt cheeses with milk in double boiler or over medium heat until cheeses are melted. Add salt, pepper, and parsley. Stir into the macaroni and serve.

Comment: Meat may be omitted.

Egg Noodles and Pasta

1 egg plus 3 egg yolks
3 tablespoons cold, filtered water
1 teaspoon sea salt
2 cups unbleached flour
Mix all ingredients. Roll out and cut into desired size noodles or run through a pasta machine.

Suggestion: Durum flour is the best to use for noodles and pasta.

Spaetzle

3 cups unbleached flour
3 teaspoons sea salt, divided
1/8 teaspoon nutmeg
3 eggs
3/4 cup milk
2 quarts filtered water
3 tablespoons butter
1/3 cup fine homemade bread crumbs

Combine flour, 1 teaspoon salt, and nutmeg. Whisk together eggs and milk. Gradually add to dry ingredients. Let stand 10 minutes. Divide dough into 3 parts. Place on a well floured board. Flatten to 1/4 inch thick. Cut into four 1/8-inch strips.

Boil 2 quarts water with remaining 2 teaspoons salt in a dutch oven. Drop dough into boiling water and simmer for 5 minutes or until spaetzle (noodle type dumpling) comes to the surface. Remove with a slotted spoon. Melt butter in a skillet over medium heat. Add dumplings and sauté 2 minutes on each side or until golden brown. Sprinkle with bread crumbs. Serve immediately.

Alfredo Sauce

4 ounces crumbled blue cheese
1 1/2 cups half and half
1 (8 ounce) package cream cheese
1 cup natural white cheese
Heat all ingredients and pour over cooked homemade or all natural fettuccini pasta. Serve with scallops or shrimp.

Pizza/Spaghetti Sauce

2 quarts ripe tomatoes
2 cloves garlic, pressed
1 jalapeno (optional)
1 onion, chopped
1 teaspoon oregano or 1 teaspoon marjoram
1 teaspoon Italian seasoning
1 teaspoon basil
1/4 cup unbleached sugar
1/4 cup canola oil
1 (6 ounce) can tomato paste
1 tablespoon sea salt

Process tomatoes, garlic, pepper, and onion in a blender or food processor. Cook on medium high for 1 hour stirring often. Add oregano, Italian seasoning, basil, sugar, oil, tomato paste, and salt. Cook for 30 minutes. Use for pizza or spaghetti.

Pizza Dough

1 cup warm filtered water
1/4 teaspoon unbleached sugar
1 package yeast
3 cups unbleached flour
1 teaspoon sea salt
1 1/2 tablespoons virgin olive oil

Put water, sugar, and yeast in bowl. Let dissolve and begin to froth. Combine flour and salt. Add yeast mixture and oil. Mix until it forms a ball. Knead on floured board until dough does not stick to hands. Let sit until double in size, approximately 40 minutes. Knead and let rise 30 minutes or until double. Knead and let sit 5 minutes. Roll out to fit pizza pan. Top with desired topping.

Toppings: pizza/spaghetti sauce; slightly fried hamburger, drained; cracklings (ground); sliced red pepper; sliced green pepper; sweet onion slices; mushrooms; home smoked bacon, ham, pineapple; and mozzarella cheese

Veggie Pizza

1 package yeast
½ cup warm filtered water
½ cup scalded milk
3 cups unbleached flour
2 tablespoons canola oil
1 teaspoon sea salt
1 teaspoon unbleached sugar

Dissolve yeast in warm water. Add lukewarm milk to 1 cup flour. Stir in yeast mixture, oil, salt, and sugar. Add remaining flour and knead until dough does not stick to your hands. Let rise. Knead down twice. Roll out and place on a 12x15-inch greased pan or a large pizza pan. Bake at 375° for 12 minutes. Cool completely. Add topping.

Topping:
Mix 1 (8 ounce) package softened cream cheese and ¼ cup mayonnaise. Spread on baked and cooled crust. Add your choice of vegetables. Chopped sweet onion, chopped broccoli, chopped cauliflower, chopped celery, diced carrots, diced red, and green peppers are recommended. Top with shredded natural Cheddar cheese or mozzarella. Cut into individual pieces and serve.

Main Dishes

Seafood

Broiled Halibut

Buttermilk Battered Fish

Catfish

Creole Style Fish, Shrimp or Scallops

Mom's Recipe for Lake Perch or Walleye

Smoked Fish

Fresh Cooked Shrimp

Oven Fried Fish

Salmon Filet

Salmon Loaf

Broiled Halibut

Sprinkle filet with sea salt and pepper. Splash with lemon juice and drizzle melted butter on filet. Broil until lightly browned on both sides. Serve at once with tartar sauce, garlic bread, and cole slaw.

Tartar Sauce:
1 cup mayonnaise
1 tablespoon finely chopped dill pickle
1 tablespoon finely chopped sweet pickle
1 teaspoon snipped parsley (optional)
Combine all ingredients and serve with fish.

Hint: To make garlic bread press 2 garlic cloves and mix with 1 stick of softened butter. Spread on a loaf of homemade, French, or Italian bread that has been split in half. Remaining garlic butter can be kept in the refrigerator for up to ten days.

Suggestion: When preparing fish simmer a little vinegar on the back burner to eliminate odor. If baking fish, squeeze lemon juice on fish or set a small oven proof dish with vinegar in it in the oven with the fish.

Hint: Make a salt bag from thin fabric or two layers of cheesecloth; use this to rub salt on grill before grilling fish, the frying pan before adding oil or in roasting pans.

Buttermilk Battered Fish

1/2 cup buttermilk
1 egg
1 cup unbleached flour
1/2 teaspoon sea salt
2 dashes pepper
1/2 teaspoon baking powder
1 pound fish fillet

Combine buttermilk, egg, flour, salt, pepper, and baking powder. Dip fish in batter. Allow excess to drain. Deep fry at 375° for 2 minutes. Turn. Fry 2 more minutes or until done or light brown. Serve with tartar sauce.

Variation: Self Rising Fish Batter: Mix 1 cup unbleached flour, 1/2 teaspoon baking powder, 1 teaspoon sea salt, 1 egg, and 1 cup filtered water. Clean fish fillet, shrimp, clams, vegetables, or onion rings. Pat dry. Dip into mixture; deep fry at 375° until light brown.

Catfish

1/8 cup buttermilk
2 tablespoons milk
1/2 teaspoon sea salt
3 tablespoons mustard
4 catfish filets
1 cup ground pecans

Combine buttermilk, milk, salt, and mustard. Dip filets in the milk mixture then into the ground pecans. Place on greased cookie sheet and bake at 500° for 12 minutes. Time may vary depending on the size of the filet. Serve with tartar sauce.

Tartar Sauce:
1 cup mayonnaise
2 tablespoons homemade sweet pickle relish
1 teaspoon chopped dill weed (optional)

Creole Style Fish, Shrimp, or Scallops

Fresh fish filet, shrimp, or scallops
1 tablespoon butter
1/4 cup minced onion
1 tablespoon finely chopped green pepper
1 tablespoon finely chopped red pepper
1/4 cup chopped celery
3 teaspoons unbleached sugar
1/4 teaspoons oregano
1 teaspoon sea salt
1 tablespoons Worcestershire sauce
1/8 teaspoon pepper
1 cup chopped tomato

Place filet, shrimp, or scallops in a lightly greased baking dish. Melt butter in a skillet. Cook and stir in onion, green and red pepper, and celery. Stir in remaining ingredients. Spoon mixture over fish and bake at 350° for 20 minutes.

Hint: Freeze fresh fish in water to keep it fresh. Thaw fish in milk. Do not thaw fish completely. This will help prevent mushiness. Wash fish in apple cider vinegar and water.

Mom's Recipe for Lake Perch or Walleye

Mix equal amounts of corn meal and bread crumbs (from homemade bread). Stir in 1 teaspoon sea salt. Dip fish or shrimp in buttermilk then into the crumbs. Layer on a wax paper lined container. Separate each layer with waxed paper. Cover and refrigerate overnight. Fry fast in hot oil.

Smoked Fish

Coat fish filet with sea salt and let stand for 1 1/2 hours. It is important that fish does not stand for les than 1 1/2 hours. Rinse and smear with brown sugar smear. Smoke according to directions on the smoker.

Brown Sugar Smear: Mix 1 cup brown sugar with a little filtered water.

Variation: Sprinkle filet with lemon pepper and smoke.

Fresh Cooked Shrimp

Clean shrimp by soaking in apple cider vinegar water. Remove veins with nutcracker pick. Rinse deveined shrimp under running water. Place shrimp in lemon water; rinse and drain. Cook in 2 quarts of filtered water with 2 teaspoons sea salt, and 1 tablespoon lemon juice. Cook until shrimp turns pink. This should take 4 to 7 minutes depending on the size of the shrimp. Serve with cocktail sauce.

Cocktail Sauce:
Mix 3/4 cup catsup, 3 tablespoons horseradish sauce, 2 teaspoons Worcestershire sauce, 2 tablespoons lemon juice, 1/2 teaspoon minced onion, and 1/4 teaspoon sea salt.

Oven Fried Fish

2 tablespoons lemon juice
1 clove garlic, pressed
2 tablespoons chicken broth
1 cup bread crumbs (from homemade bread)
1/2 teaspoon sea salt
1/2 teaspoon white pepper
1 pound fish fillet
2 teaspoons olive oil

Grease a pan large enough to hold the amount of fish you wish to prepare. In a separate dish, combine lemon juice, garlic, and broth. In another dish mix bread crumbs, salt, and pepper. Dip filet into lemon juice and broth mixture; and into the bread crumb mixture. Place into the greased pan and bake at 450° for 10 minutes or until done.

Salmon Filet

3 tablespoons snipped parsley
3 tablespoons grated orange peel
1 tablespoon unbleached sugar
1 teaspoon sea salt
1 teaspoon pepper
6 (6 ounce) salmon filet
1 tablespoon butter
1 tablespoon canola oil

Combine parsley, orange peel, sugar, salt, and pepper. Roll filet in mixture. Melt butter and oil in frying pan. Place filet in hot fat and fry for 4 minutes on each side or until done and golden brown. Serve with fish sauce.

Optional: Fish Sauce:
Fry 1 chopped sweet onion in 1/4 cup butter. Blend 3 tablespoons unbleached flour, 1 tablespoon mustard, 1/2 teaspoon sea salt, 1/4 teaspoon pepper, 1 1/4 cups chicken broth and 1 cup half and half. Stir and boil 1 minute. Serve over fish.

Suggestion: Use leftover salmon to make salmon patties. Crumble salmon and add 1 egg and 1/4 cup bread crumbs. Form into patties and fry in hot oil until brown on both sides.